RAINY DAY PASTIMES

contents

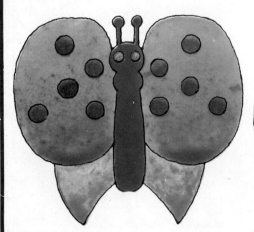
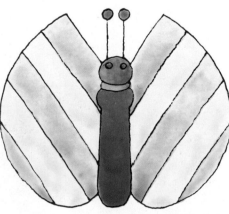

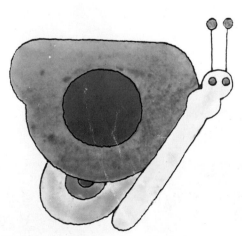

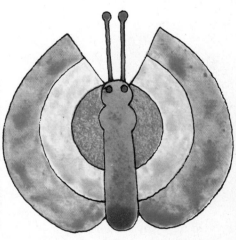

Edited by Magda Gray and Yvonne Deutch

Photographs
Michael Boys: 56-57 (top)
Camera Press: 44-45 (centre), 71, 76
Susan Griggs Agency/photo Monique
Jacot: 7
John Hillelson Agency: 38
Wendy Kay: 16, 43 (inset), 56 (bottom),
57 (centre, bottom left and right),
64-65
Chris Lewis: 79
Neil Lorimer: 10, 20, 21, 26-27, 30-31,
36, 37, 48-49, 52, 66
L'Escargot: Matisse/Tate Gallery,
London-photo John Webb: 44 (top left)
Ethne Reuss: 44 (bottom left) 45 (right)
Bill Mclaughlin: 79, 84, 85
ZEFA: 35, 43

Published by Marshall Cavendish
Publications Limited
58, Old Compton Street
London W1V 5PA

©Marshall Cavendish Limited,
1973-1975

Most of this material was first published
by Marshall Cavendish Limited in the
special *175 Ideas to Keep Children Happy*

This volume first printed 1975

ISBN 0 85685 137 X

Printed in Great Britain by
The Artisan Press Ltd.

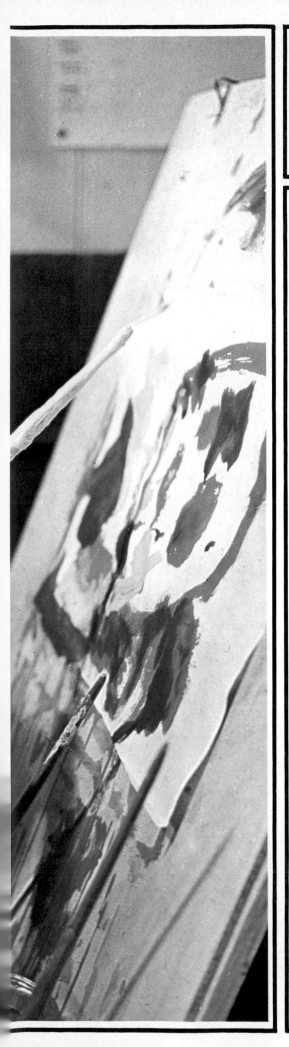

introduction

On days when the weather keeps everyone indoors, children and grown-ups can easily get bored. When this happens, and nobody can think of anything which is fun and different to do, don't despair Here's a bright, happy, friendly book, crammed full of ideas which can turn a dull day into a brand new adventure. There are 215 marvellous pastimes to keep everyone happy, and they are designed to cater to all sorts of different moods and occasions.

The choice is enormous—with lovely things to make: jewellery, toy animals, paper lanterns, paper flowers, a garage and a robot. There are super games too, which can be noisy or quiet, dressing up ideas, indoor and outdoor gardening, simple cooking, exciting collages to make, gifts for Christmas and Easter, ideas for make-believe and hilarious party games like 'silly tea' and 'musical dressing'. When the sun comes out for a while, the section on things to do outdoors is full of exciting suggestions. Even car journeys are catered for, with a host of special games to play while travelling.

Everyone will love the pretty illustrations, and there are lots of amusing drawings. Also, most of the materials used are common household items, and are easily available. The instructions are very easy to follow, and each game or task has a special symbol to indicate which age group it is most suitable for. Days indoors need never be a problem again with this helpful book in the home.

a word to grown-ups

No child has an endless supply of things to do; no parent has a limitless fount of suggestions. This book is designed to bridge the gap when child and parent run out of ideas at the same time; to keep a child—or children—occupied, and happy doing something creative, constructive, interesting or just downright enjoyable. Some things you may not have thought of, some things you may not have heard of, some things you may have forgotten from your own childhood.

The things to do are grouped under general headings—indoors, outdoors, quiet, noisy, messy, etc. None of these should be interpreted too literally because what is an absorbing and deathly silent occupation for one child can be an ear-splitting riot for another; and some children have the incredible knack of making everything they do messy. The things the child will do alone are written to be read to him or her, with warning asides to parents where necessary. The things the child will do in the company of adults—party games, things to do while travelling—are addressed to the parent who will supervise proceedings. The best way to use this book is simply to flip through it until you find something suitable. To save your time and your temper, however, don't suggest something similar to what the child has already been doing. And if you're frantically busy don't suggest something that is going to involve you every other minute. On the other hand, it is unreasonable to expect the child to start something completely new without your help. A few minutes spent gathering together the things the child is going to need and showing him or her what to do is well-invested time, no matter how busy you are. Some children are blessed with a reasonable amount of patience; others don't appear to have any. Either way, they need to move from one thing to another. The way to get them involved is to impose as few limitations as possible—let them be free to use their imaginations. If they want to do something differently, in their own way, allow them to go ahead. Rigid rules restrict both enjoyment and creativity.

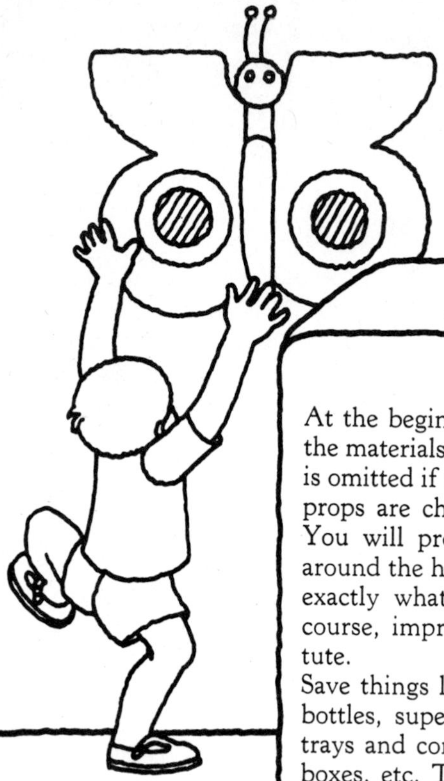

Ages

As a quick visual guide each game or suggestion has the following symbol which indicates what age range it is suitable for.

●   under 5 years old

▲   5 years to 7 years old

■   over 7 years old

This is not a rigid categorization. Obviously some children will prefer more complicated ideas while others will like to take a simple suggestion and adapt it to suit themselves. If you are the parent then you will know what sort of things your child is interested in. But if the child is not yours you may find it useful to be able to see at a glance what would be a suitable suggestion.

You will need . . .

At the beginning of each game we list the materials required. (This paragraph is omitted if nothing is needed.) All the props are cheap and readily available. You will probably have lots of them around the house and if you don't have exactly what we suggest you can, of course, improvise a reasonable substitute.

Save things like yogurt cartons, plastic bottles, supermarket polystyrene meat trays and containers, empty cardboard boxes, etc. These all have tremendous play potential, as do some of the staple elements of the average kitchen store-cupboard. If you stop thinking about food simply as something to eat, and reconsider it as something your children can play with, all kinds of possibilities open up.

Tracing and transferring

Any thin paper which is sufficiently transparent can be used as tracing paper provided the picture which is to be traced is bold enough.

To transfer the picture to another sheet of paper, first lightly trace the picture, then turn the tracing paper over and, using a soft-lead pencil, run over the lines again, pressing hard with the pencil. Now place the tracing paper on to a sheet of clean white paper with the heavy lines downwards. Holding the two sheets of paper together, rub gently over the picture with the soft-lead pencil. When you have covered all the lines, lift the tracing paper clear and the picture will now be transferred on to the white paper.

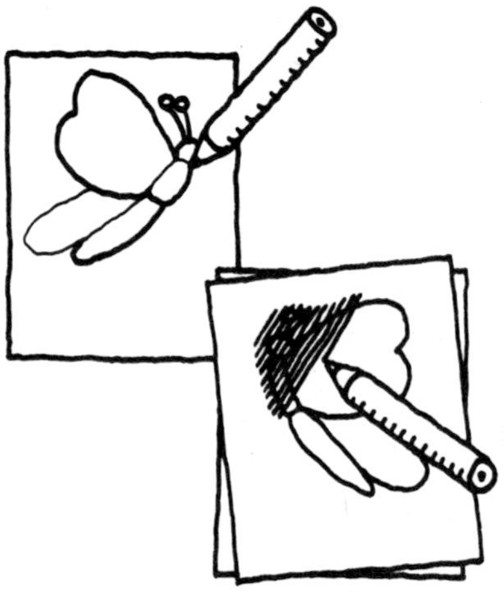

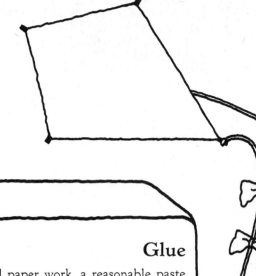

Glue

For all paper work, a reasonable paste that won't harm young children can be made by mixing flour and water with a pinch of salt until it is thick and gooey. If you make it a little thinner, more like cream, and simmer it on a stove for five minutes, it will stick better.

Paint

The best paint for children is powdered poster paint. It is cheap, comes in good strong colours and all you have to do is add water—using more or less according to how thick you want the paint to be. Added advantages are that it will take on most materials and washes off hands and faces easily.

Don'ts

Don't let small children use things like needles, pins or small buttons which they might swallow.

Don't allow young children—particularly if they suck their fingers—to handle rubber-based glues, lead-based paints, or anything with an obvious toxic or chemical base which could be poisonous or cause ill effects if swallowed. If they are required (e.g. the chemicals in the water garden, No. 53) handle them yourself or supervise the child closely.

Don't give young children live matches —give them used ones or cut the match-heads off.

Don't let young children play with plastic bags. They are dangerous.

Don't allow young children to play with water alone. They can drown in one foot of water just as easily as in six feet.

Don't let children use sharp scissors (blunt-ended paper-scissors are easily obtainable and safe), hammers, nails, or sharp knives unless you are there to supervise them. Even sharp hard-lead pencils can be dangerous if the point breaks off under the child's skin.

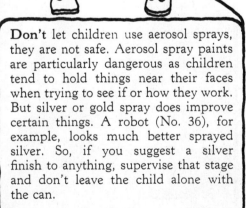

Don't let children use aerosol sprays, they are not safe. Aerosol spray paints are particularly dangerous as children tend to hold things near their faces when trying to see if or how they work. But silver or gold spray does improve certain things. A robot (No. 36), for example, looks much better sprayed silver. So, if you suggest a silver finish to anything, supervise that stage and don't leave the child alone with the can.

quiet things to do indoors

Everything made from the ideas in this section can be as crude or as complicated as the child's ability dictates—the end result will give equal satisfaction.

Paper, crayons, scissors and glue can be used to make simple fans and darts or more complicated cut out hand-in-hand people. If you add assorted cardboard boxes to the list some quite sophisticated things can be made.

Coloured tissue paper, straws, egg-boxes, paper cups and match-boxes are the staple commodities for making flowers and animals. All children like this kind of creative play, making something themselves which bears a recognizable resemblance to reality.

Pipe cleaners are perhaps the most versatile things to make animals with. They are very cheap, and have endless possibilities because they can be bent into any shape. Most children, even the very young ones, should be able to make their own people and animals satisfactorily with pipe cleaners.

You'll find more quiet things to do under 'Messy things to do indoors' (Nos. 68-84). The suggestions in this section should not—unless you are unlucky—turn out to be messy.

Jigsaws
●▲

You will need: old magazines, thin cardboard or stiff paper, scissors and glue.

Tear out full-page colour pictures or advertisements from old magazines. Get some thin cardboard or stiff paper and some glue. Stick one picture on each piece of cardboard and then cut it up with squiggly lines. For a real challenge, mix up three or four home-made jigsaws or stick a picture on each side of the card so that you have a double-sided jigsaw.

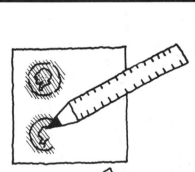

Play money
▲

You will need: three or four coins, a thin sheet of paper, soft pencil, scissors and glue.

Take three or four coins and put them under a thin sheet of paper. Then rub a soft pencil all over the paper so that the pattern of the coin appears. Do as many as you can, then stick the paper to thin cardboard and cut out the play money. For a professional job, take a rubbing of both sides of the coin and stick it to each side of the cardboard.

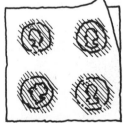

Paper-weight
▲■

You will need: a large flat stone about the size of a big potato, paper, glue, tiny pebbles and clear varnish.

To make your stone into an attractive paper-weight decorate it with lots of tiny pebbles (or, if you are by the seaside, with tiny shells). Clean both the big pebble and the 'decoration', then stand the pebble flat on a piece of paper and cover the top and sides thickly with a strong glue. Press the shells into the glue putting them very close together, then wait until it is dry and cover the whole thing with an aerosol-spray clear varnish.

(Parents should supervise this final stage as it is dangerous to allow children to handle aerosol sprays on their own.)

Paper lanterns ▲

You will need: paper, scissors and glue.

Fold an oblong sheet of paper in half, then make equal cuts from the folded edge, taking care not to snip right across the paper. Open it out and glue the edges together, then cut a small strip of paper for the handle and glue it to each side at the top. If you want to colour it, it's best to do so before you open it out.

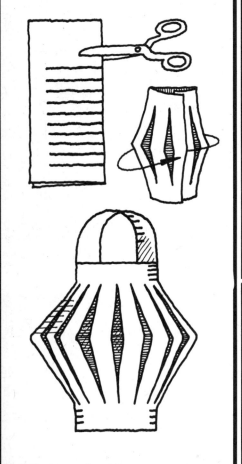

Paper darts ▲

You will need: paper.

Fold an oblong sheet of paper in half lengthwise. Fold each side over to the crease diagonally, twice or three times, then fold it back along the crease.

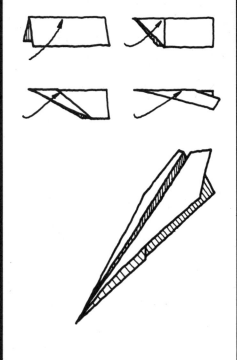

Making a fan ●▲

You will need: paper, scissors and glue.

Pleat a piece of paper making each pleat about half an inch wide. Stick a thin strip of paper around one end of the folded paper, then open out the other end.

To make a patterned fan, cut little notches in the paper while it is still folded—taking care not to cut right across the paper.

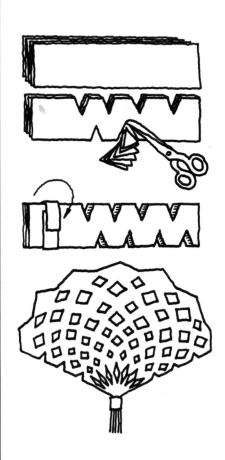

Hand-in-hand people ■

You will need: a thin sheet of paper, crayons and scissors.

Fold a thin sheet of paper into pleats. Draw an outline of a man or woman on the top surface so that the hands disappear off the sides of the paper. Cut around the outline and open it out. Draw in the face and clothes of each of the people and colour them.

Fortune teller

▲■

You will need: a square piece of paper and a pencil.

Take a square piece of paper and fold it in half twice. Open it up and fold the four corners into the middle, using the creases as guide lines. Turn the square over and fold the four corners into the middle again. Letter each of the eight triangles A–H, then lift each flap in turn and write a fortune underneath. (e.g. You will be lucky today. You will be invited to a party.) Pull out the four flaps on the underside and you will have four little cones to put your fingers in. To tell a fortune, ask someone to choose a number and then move your fingers together and apart that number of times. The person then has to choose one letter from the four you can see when you have finished counting, and whatever you have written under this letter is his or her fortune.

Paper hand puppets

▲■

You will need: a square piece of paper and crayons.

Using the 'fortune teller' method of folding the paper you can make hand puppets in the form of animals' faces by painting eyes or noses on to the two top triangles, sticking on whiskers, etc. The puppet is worked by holding the top two cones together and moving the lower cones up and down to make it talk.

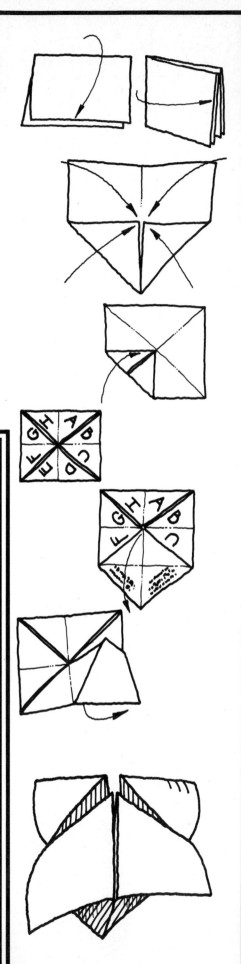

Zig-zag book

▲

You will need: thin cardboard, old magazines and crayons.

Fold a long strip of thin cardboard in half then in half again back on itself. Unfold it loosely so that it stands up on one edge. Each of the four 'pages' can be filled in with a different picture—cut pictures out of magazines, or stick in some drawings of your family.

Paper patterns

●▲

You will need: thin paper, scissors and wax crayons.

Fold a large sheet of thin paper in half as many times as you can. Cut off the corners and make any other cuts you feel like. Open out the sheet and colour the pattern.

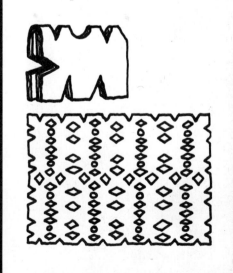

Sausage dog ▲

You will need: an empty toilet paper roll, thick yellow wool, paper, glue, scissors and crayons.

You can make this dog with the cardboard tube inside a toilet roll, some thick yellow wool and a piece of paper. Glue a circle of paper over one end of the roll and draw the dog's face on it. Then bind the roll with the wool, cut off a few lengths for the fringe and glue them round the face. If there is any wool left over, glue on a bushy tail at the other end.

Sheep ▲

You will need: an empty match-box, used wooden matches, sticky tape, glue, absorbent cotton wool and cardboard.

Use an empty match-box for the body and used wooden matches for the legs. Stick these in each corner by wrapping the box with sticky tape. Glue absorbent cotton wool over the match-box to make his woolly coat. Cut his head and neck from a piece of cardboard and stick it into place.

Wriggly snake ●▲

You will need: wooden cotton reels [thread spools], string and paint.

Collect together as many old cotton reels [thread spools] as you can find and thread them together on a piece of string. Tie a big knot at each end to hold them on, then paint each reel a different colour and paint a face on one end.

Tortoise ▲

You will need: scissors, cardboard, crayons, an empty egg-shell and green paint.

Cut the shape of a tortoise—four thick legs, little tail and bulbous head—from a piece of cardboard and bend it into shape so that it stands on its legs and the head looks up.

Draw on the tortoise's eyes and toes and paint him green. To make his shell, clean an empty egg-shell, crush it into small pieces and stick them on to the tortoise's back. Then give it a second coat of green paint.

Hedgehog

●▲

You will need: a lump of plasticine or modelling clay, scissors and straws. Mould the plasticine or modelling clay into the rough shape of your hedgehog, give his little face a nice pointed nose and two eyes, then make his prickles by cutting the straws into short lengths and pushing them in all over his body.

Egg-box animals

●▲

You will need: egg-boxes, scissors, paint, buttons, glue, cardboard, string, wool, paper, pencil and sticky tape. Ordinary egg-boxes can be made into all sorts of animals. Here are a few ideas to get you started.
For a convincing **caterpillar,** cut out a strip of cones and paint them green with yellow stripes or dots. An old button stuck on each side at one end make good eyes.

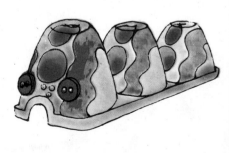

Two cones, painted a brownish-yellow, will make the back of a **camel.** Stick on cardboard legs in each corner and cut the head from a piece of cardboard. It can be stuck on to the body or slotted into a slit cut in one end. A piece of string with a knot in the end serves for a tail.

For a creepy-crawly **snake,** cut up separate cones and thread them together with string. Paint them different colours, or in stripes, and leave a short length of string at each end for the tongue and tail.

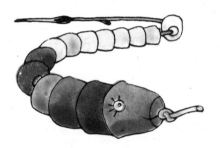

To make a **lion,** use an egg-box with six cones and cut out the middle two. Stand it upside down and you have the body of the lion with four legs. To make the face, use a circle of stiff cardboard. Stick it on to the body and paint the face. For the lion's mane cut up short lengths of wool, yellow if possible, and stick them all round the face.

For a fat little **pig,** stick two cones together with sticky tape. You can make legs from cardboard or used wooden matches, either sticking them to the body or slotting them in. To make the curly tail, wrap a thin strip of paper round a pencil, leave it for a while so that it curls, then fix it to the back of the pig with sticky tape. Cut the floppy ears from another piece of paper and stick them into place, then draw the pig's face and paint him pink.

Melon seed necklace

▲■

You will need: melon or pumpkin seeds, a needle, strong thread and some paint.

If you save the seeds from a melon or pumpkin and wash and dry them they make a good necklace, but they have to be pierced with a needle.

Thread the needle with strong thread and knot it at one end, then string the seeds by pushing the needle through the end of each one.

The easiest way to colour the seeds is to dip the necklace into a pot of paint and then hang it up to dry. But they look quite good unpainted, as well. Practically anything that you can thread string through—macaroni, straws, old buttons, and so on—can be used to make necklaces and bracelets.

Macaroni can be painted and goes nice dull shades.

Straws are more difficult to colour, but you can buy them in different colours then cut them into short lengths and thread them on to string or wool. Instead of straws, you could roll sheets of paper around a pencil, glue them along the side, colour them and cut them up in the same way.

For a really exotic creation, alternate the pieces of straw with circles cut from aluminium foil or cleaned silver or gold milk bottle-tops.

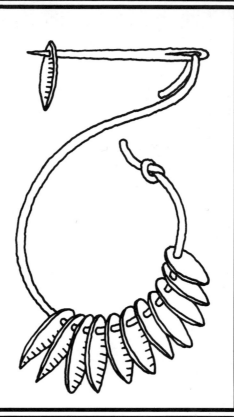

Rings

▲

You will need: stiff paper, glue, paint and a few small decorations.

Cut a small strip of stiff paper and glue it into a ring. Paint it or glue on the same decoration suggested for brooches.

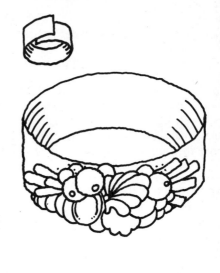

Brooches

▲■

You will need: stiff cardboard, a safety pin, sticky tape, crayons, glue and a few small decorations.

Cut the cardboard in the shape of a flower and then colour and decorate the petals for extra effect. For decoration you can glue on small shells, silver balls and tiny multi-coloured sprinkles —both used for cake decoration—or even rice (it can be painted).

Finally, fix the safety pin to the back of the brooch with sticky tape.

A vegetable necklace (left) made of carrots, radishes and green beans is so pretty that it really does not matter that it will only last a day or two.

Earrings

●

You will need: tissue paper and some wool.

Cherries on double stalks make marvellous earrings but they are not available throughout the year. You can, however, copy the idea by using a piece of wool instead of the stalks and woollen or tissue paper tassels instead of cherries.

Crinoline lady
▲■

You will need: stiff paper, scissors, glue, paint and a straw.

Cut two circles from stiff paper. One must be about 8 inches across, the other about 5 inches. Cut scallops round the edge of the larger circle and a fringe round the smaller one, then make a straight cut from the edge to the centre of each circle. (To find the centre, lightly fold the circle in half twice—the centre is where the folds cross.)

Overlap and glue the edges of each circle. The tall cone makes the lady and the smaller one her parasol. Cut a small circle for her head, leaving a small tab underneath, and draw her face. Snip the point of the bigger cone off, slot in the tab on her head and glue it into place.

Paint the lady, her long dress and her parasol. With a straw, make the handle of the parasol, then glue one end of the handle to her hands and the other inside the parasol.

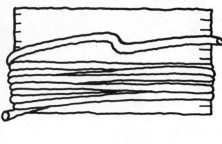

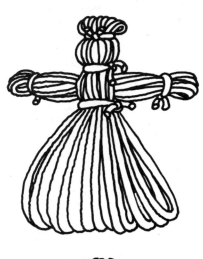

Wool dolls
▲■

You will need: cardboard, wool, scissors and a needle and thread.

You need a piece of cardboard about 10 inches long by 7 inches wide and a ball of wool.

First wrap the wool about a dozen times around the width of the cardboard, slip it off and tie it together about half an inch from each end. This will make the doll's arms.

Next wrap the wool around the length of the card about twice as many times as you did for the arms, slip it off and tie it right at the top and again an inch lower—this will be the head. Slip the arms through the long body loops underneath the head and tie again under the arms to keep them secure.

Cut the top loops to make the doll's hair and sew on eyes, nose and mouth for the face. If you want a girl doll, cut the bottom strands and fluff them out for her skirt. If you want a boy, tie the wool at the bottom of his body, separate the strands to make two legs and tie them again at the feet.

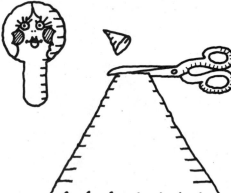

Flower pressing ▲■

You will need: flowers, blotting paper and some heavy books.

Wild flowers are usually prettiest for pressing. Choose simple flowers with petals that will lie flat—heavy, bulbous flowers do not press well. Press the flowers as soon as possible after picking, and keep them in water until you are ready to use them.

To press the flowers, lay a sheet of blotting-paper on top of one book and arrange a few flowers on it. Arrange the petals and leaves so that they are flat, then cover the flowers with another sheet of blotting-paper and pile half a dozen heavy books on top. Leave them undisturbed for five or six days and then they are ready to use.

Pressed flowers will make a fascinating scrap-book if they are carefully stuck down with sticky tape and labelled. They can also be used for pretty floral pictures. Find a piece of stiff cardboard of the size you want, then cut out a piece of felt or coloured paper in the shape of a vase and stick this on to the card. Finally, stick the flowers into position with a little glue—arranging them so that they look as if they are standing in the vase. To protect the flowers cover the picture with a piece of cellophane or plastic and glue it down at the back of the cardboard.

French knitting ■

You will need: an empty cotton reel [thread spool], four small nails, a hammer, a thin knitting-needle and various coloured wools.

This makes a knitted cord which you can sew into a flat mat or use as a belt. Four small nails must be hammered into the top of an empty wooden cotton reel [thread spool]. (Parents should do this.) Thread the wool down through the hole in the reel and then around the nails as shown in the picture. With the thin knitting-needle pull the wool over the nails. Tie more wool of different colours as you need it. The cord comes out through the bottom of the reel. You can make it as short or as long as you like, but remember always to finish it off with a knot to stop it becoming unravelled.

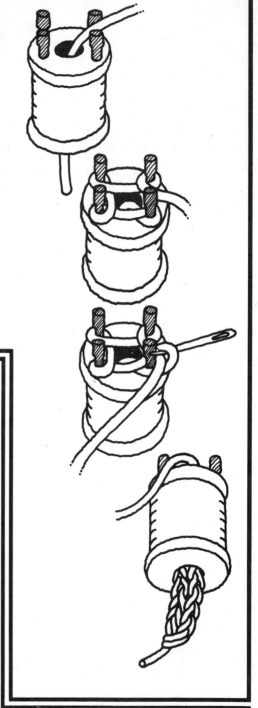

Woolly pompons ▲■

You will need: stiff cardboard, a jam-jar, coin, pencil, needle, wool and scissors.

Draw two circles on to a piece of stiff cardboard using the bottom of a jam-jar as a guideline. Next take a coin and use it to draw two circles in the centre of each of the cardboard pieces, then cut out the inner circle. Put the two circles together and start winding a length of wool round and round as neatly as you can. Tie on more wool of different colours whenever necessary and carry on until the inner hole has disappeared. (Use a needle to pull the last few lengths through.)

Now very carefully cut around the edge of the wool circle between the two pieces of cardboard. When all the strands are cut tie a length of wool tightly between the cardboard circles. Cut away the cardboard and fluff out the wool.

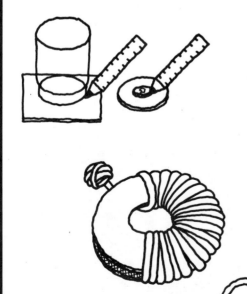

Paper pansies

You will need: small squares of coloured tissue paper, a pencil, scissors and coloured or painted pipe cleaners.

Fold each square in half twice and draw a petal shape on one side of the folded tissue. Cut around the shape and open it out.

Take two shapes of different colours and make a small hole in the centre of each one. Push a pipe cleaner through the holes and bend the cleaner back to hold the petals in place.

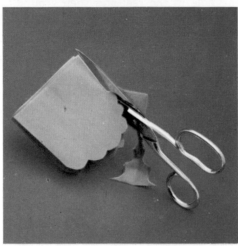

Paper cup sunflowers

●▲

You will need: paper cups, scissors, paint, sticky tape and straws, pipe cleaners or pencils.

These are the easiest of all flowers to make. Simply make a number of cuts from the rim to the base of a paper cup and then open it out. The bottom of the cup makes the centre of the flower and the cut strips are the petals. Paint the flowers in any colours available. Stalks can be made from straws, pipe cleaners or even pencils pushed through holes cut in the centres of the flowers and stuck underneath with sticky tape.

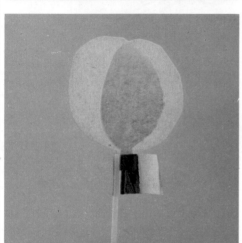

Tissue tulips

▲

You will need: coloured tissue paper, glue or thread and yogurt or cottage cheese cartons.

Small pieces of coloured tissue paper tied or stuck to the ends of straws create simple and colourful flowers. The tissue paper can be crumpled or shaped like tulips.

'Vases' can be made from old yogurt or cottage cheese cartons covered in different coloured tissue papers.

Buttonholes

●▲

You will need: coloured paper handkerchiefs, scissors, thread or wool and sticky tape.

Paper carnations can be made from coloured paper handkerchiefs. Cut the handkerchief in half, lengthwise, so that you have a thin strip. Fold it like an accordion, then tie it in the middle with a piece of thread or wool. Fluff out the folds on one end of the tissue and bind the other side with sticky tape to make the stalk.

For a really convincing buttonhole, cut two or three green tissue paper leaves and fix them behind the flower.

31 Cotton reel [thread spool] tanks

▲■

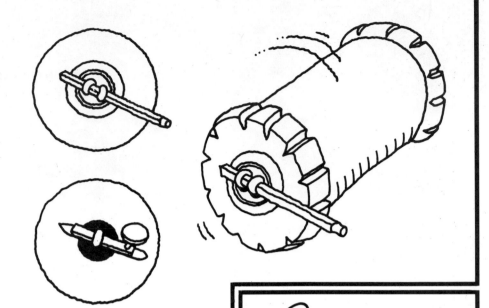

You will need: a cotton reel [thread spool], a strong elastic band, two wooden matchsticks and a button or thin 'slice' of a candle.

Victorian children first played with this wonderful home-made toy—the self-propelled cotton reel [thread spool]. To make it push the elastic band through the hole in the centre of the wooden reel and anchor it at one end with a short piece of matchstick. Make a little groove for the match or jam it with a pin. Thread the button or candle slice on to the other end of the elastic band and then slip a full length wooden matchstick through the loop. Wind it up at the button end, making sure the long matchstick overlaps the edge of the cotton reel, then put it on the floor and watch it run!

One of the good things about this toy is that it is very easy to make and offers limitless scope for the imagination. If you have little notches filed into the two rims of the reel, it becomes a very passable tank and will climb fairly steep inclines. And for further sophistication you can make paper covers (in the shape of buses, cars or trucks) to slip over the reel and have self-propelled cars, while as a 'breakdown vehicle' it will tow small model cars. Finally, if you have more than one, they are good for races.

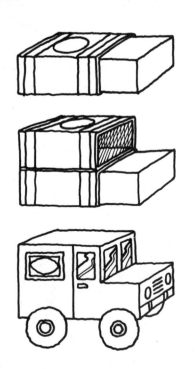

32 Match-box traffic

●▲

You will need: small match-boxes, glue, scissors, the tube from a toilet paper roll, stiff cardboard, paper and paint.

Small match-boxes have endless possibilities for making models of cars, trucks and vehicles of all kinds. The simplest way to make a car is to slide the tray of one match-box half out to form the front, then stick another match-box on top for the cab. Cover it with paper and paint on the doors, windows and lights, etc. Cut the wheels out of stiff cardboard and stick them in position. From that basic design you can create almost any sort of vehicle, given enough glue and match-boxes. Toilet paper roll tubes are very good for making the tank part of tankers, for example, and an ordinary match-box tray with two wheels stuck on each side makes a good trailer.

33 Twizzlers

▲

You will need: stiff cardboard, scissors, crayons and string.

Cut out a circle of stiff cardboard (the centre of a paper plate is fine) and decorate it with bright colours.

Make two holes close to the centre and thread a loop of string through them. Hold one end of the loop in each hand and swing the card over and over to wind it up. Then tighten and slacken the string to make it spin.

34   Garage ●

You will need: a cardboard box, scissors and paint.

Almost any old cardboard box will make a good garage. Cut the lid off completely, then cut doors out from the sides—not too many, or the box will not stand up properly. With felt-tip pens or poster paint, colour it all over and then draw on the petrol pumps, the sign, windows and anything else you like to add.

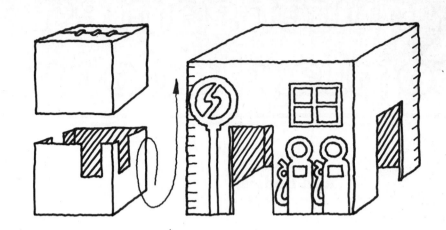

35   Moon landing ▲

You will need: egg-boxes, scissors, a large sheet of cardboard, glue, egg-shells, paint, cardboard tube, aluminium foil.

Egg-boxes can be made to look surprisingly like the surface of the moon. Collect together as many as possible, cut them up and glue them on to a large sheet of flat cardboard. Make the surface as irregular as possible. Cut the tops off some of the cones and stick them back on the other way round to form craters. (The jagged edges of empty egg-shells might help to make your landscape bleak and uninviting.) Paint the whole surface grey, or a combination of grey and black, when everything is stuck on to it.

To make a rocket, stick the cone of an egg-box to one end of a cardboard tube. (The tube from a toilet paper roll or paper towel roll is fine.) Make short cuts round the edge on the other end and bend the edges outward so that it stands firmly, then cover it all with aluminium foil.

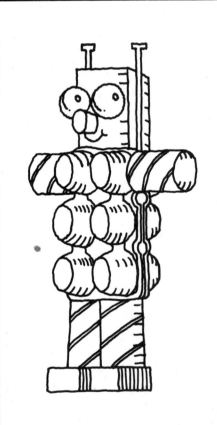

36   Robot ■

You will need: two egg-boxes, two match-boxes, cardboard tubes, glue, two ping-pong balls, a cork, two screw-in hooks, two knitting-needles and some paint.

Glue the two egg-boxes together to make the robot's body, glue match-box feet to his cardboard tube legs and glue them to his body. Two thinner pieces of tube, sticking straight out, make the arms. This robot has got a large match-box head, two ping-pong balls for eyes, a cork for a nose, knitting-needles as antennae and screw-in hooks for hands. But, starting with the egg-box body, it should be easy to improvise the rest of him with whatever materials you have. Once he is painted all over he will look convincing enough.

quiet games to play indoors

Heads and bodies
●▲

You will need: pencils and thin strips of paper.

This drawing game is guaranteed fun for any number of players. Each player is given a thin strip of paper and a pencil. On the top of the paper, the player draws a funny face and a neck and folds the paper back so that only a little of the neck is showing. When everyone has drawn a face, the papers are passed round to the left and then a body and arms are added and again folded back so that only the bottom of the body is showing. The papers are passed round again and this time the players add legs and feet, then fold the paper so that only a blank strip at the bottom is showing. When the papers are passed round for the last time, each player thinks of a funny name and adds it to the drawing, then the papers are jumbled up. Each player takes a paper back, then they are opened up and compared together.

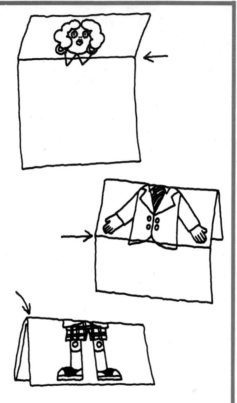

POCAHONTAS

Beetle
▲■

You will need: a dice and pencils and paper.

This is a dice game for any number of players. Apart from the dice, everyone will need a pencil and paper.

Each player takes it in turn to throw the dice and the object is to be first to complete a drawing of a beetle. You have to throw a six to start the game. Then you need to throw the following numbers to draw your beetle, which must be drawn in the order given here: a 6 for the body, 5 for the head, 4 for each of the six legs, 3 for each of the feet, 2 for each of the eyes, 1 for the nose and another 1 for the mouth.

Up Jenkins
■

You will need: a coin.

This game is for two teams seated on opposite sides of a table. One team has a coin which it has to conceal from the others.

To start the game, the team with the coin put their hands under the table and pass it between them until the leader of the other team says 'Up Jenkins!'. On this command the whole team must put up their hands, tightly clenched, on the table. It is now up to the other team to guess who has the coin.

To help them guess, they can order the team with the coin to do certain things: 'Creepy Crawly', which means moving the hands forward in a crawling movement; 'Wibbley Wobbley', turning the clenched hands over and back again; or 'Flat on the Table', laying the hands out flat.

If the player with the coin is identified, the other team take a turn to hide it; if not, the same team have another turn.

Old maid
▲

You will need: a pack of cards.

This card game is for more than two and up to six players.

The Queen of Spades is taken out and put to one side and then the whole pack is dealt out. Each player makes as many pairs as possible from the cards in his hand—two sevens, two Jacks, two Kings, etc.—and lays them down on the table, keeping the other, unmatched, cards in his hand.

Then the player on the left of the dealer offers his remaining cards face downwards to the player on his left, who takes one. If it pairs with a card in his hand, he lays the pair down then offers the cards in his hand face downwards to the player on his left, and so on round the table.

The winner is the player who has most pairs when only one card, a Queen, is left in play.

Animal snap ▲

You will need: a pack of cards.
This is a good variation of ordinary Snap for up to four children. A complete pack of cards is dealt out among the players, and they keep their cards in a pile in front of them, face downwards. Each player thinks of an animal to be—something that makes a distinctive noise—a cow perhaps.
The cards are turned up by the players in turn and laid down face upwards. As soon as a card is turned up that matches another card already showing, the players have to make the noise of their animal. The child who makes his or her noise first wins all the cards which have been turned up and the winner of the game is the one left with all the cards.

Battleships ■

You will need: pencils and paper.
This is an exciting game for two somewhat older players.
Divide four pieces of paper into at least 144 squares (twelve across and twelve down.) Number the squares along the top of the paper and letter them down the side.
Each player has two sheets of paper, one to position his own fleet and the other to mark the shots he makes at his opponent's fleet. A fleet comprises: a battleship (occupying five adjacent squares); two destroyers (three squares each); three corvettes (two squares each); and two submarines (two squares each).
When each player has positioned his own fleet—marking them in any arrangement he likes on his piece of paper without letting the other person see—they then take turns to fire at their opponent's fleet, calling out the shots by the letter and number of the square and marking them on their shot chart. Whenever a hit is made, the opponent has to say so and identify the ship. (If heated accusations of cheating are made an umpire can check the players' papers against each other.) It takes five hits to sink the battleship, three to sink the destroyer, and so on.
The winner is the one who is first to sink the other player's entire fleet.

Boxes ■

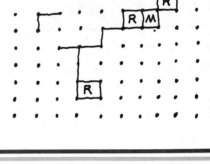

You will need: pencils and paper.
Mark a sheet of paper with ten lines of ten dots so that the dots line up and down and from side to side. The object of the game is to form boxes and the winner is the one who makes the most.
The first player draws one line joining any two dots up and down or from side to side. The second player joins another two in any place he chooses, and so on. Each player has to try to avoid joining the third side of a square and giving his or her opponent the chance to form a box.
When a player can form a box he writes his initial in it and has another go—so he may be able to make a number of boxes in one turn.

Swapping ■

You will need: three silver coins, three copper coins, pencil and paper.
Draw a row of seven boxes on a piece of paper. Put the three silver coins in the three boxes on the right and the three copper coins in the boxes on the left. The object of the game is to swap the silver coins with the copper coins in the minimum number of moves. Each coin can either move into the empty square next to it or jump one coin of the different colour provided that there is an empty space on the other side. (One piece of information, fifteen moves is the absolute minimum to solve this. See solution page.)

Separate circles ■

You will need: Seven coins, a square sheet of paper and a pencil.
Put the seven coins onto the paper in the positions shown here. The object of the game is to separate each circle by drawing only three straight lines from edge to edge of the paper.
(See solution page.)

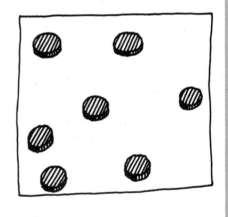

MY FLEET

ENEMY FLEET

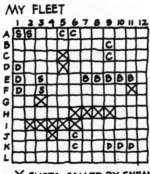

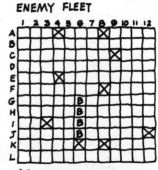

B: BATTLESHIP
D: DESTROYER
C: CORVETTE
S: SUBMARINE

X SHOTS CALLED BY ENEMY

X SHOTS CALLED BY YOU MARKING WHERE ENEMY SHIPS HAVE BEEN HIT.

indoor gardening

Children love to watch things grow and can learn a great deal about Nature by being encouraged to plant seeds and shown how to look after them. Children who live in towns benefit particularly from an indoor garden. They will need patience to wait for indoor seeds to grow, but that is a good thing to learn, too. Adults normally expect some reward from their gardening in terms of fruit or vegetable or blazing flowers; children don't—the thrill of seeing a seed sprout is sufficient.

To show that plants need light
Sprinkle some grass seed or bird seed on to a wet cloth, sponge or piece of blotting-paper. Leave it on a sunny window-sill, covered with a glass dish, and water it every day. When the seeds start shooting take away the glass cover and replace it with an ordinary plate. The seedlings will lose their colour within hours—a vivid demonstration that a plant needs light.

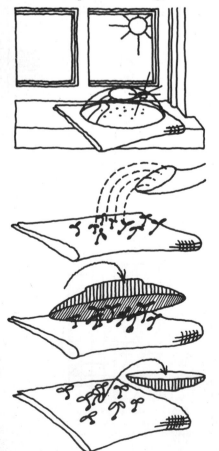

To show how a plant drinks
Fill a glass with water and red food colouring. Cut the bottom off a stalk of celery or a carrot and stand it in the water for a couple of hours. When cut open, the celery will be pink and white striped and the carrot will be bright red inside.

An indoor garden is great fun to plant and grow. This one (right) includes mustard and cress, carrot tops, avocado plant and stone, a tiny tree grown from an orange pip and a potato head with green grass hair.

Growing little trees from fruit seeds ▲

You will need: fruit seeds, a flower-pot and soil or potting compost.
Seeds from grapefruit, oranges, lemons and tangerines can all be planted. Soak the seeds in water overnight, then fill a pot with good soil from the garden, or a potting compost. Plant three or four pips about half an inch deep and keep the soil moist and the pot in a warm, light place. If you remember to water the soil regularly the seedlings will sprout in about eight weeks. (Do not water every day or you will drown the seeds; about once or twice a week is often enough). Take out all but the strongest plant and it will eventually grow into a little tree with dark, glossy leaves. (Acorns and horse chestnuts will also grow in the same way.)

Egg-shell gardens ■

You will need: empty egg-shells, an egg-box, soil or potting compost and some seeds.
Empty egg-shells make ideal containers to grow seeds in.
Clean the half-shells and fill them with soil or potting compost. (It is easiest to stand the egg-shells up in an egg-box). Keep the soil moist and when the seedlings are between one and two inches high transplant them into pots.

Pineapple plants ▲

You will need: the top of a fresh pineapple and a pot of damp, sandy soil.
Cut the top two inches off a fresh pineapple and let it dry for about a week. Put it in a pot of damp, sandy soil and keep it moist. Within a few weeks it will start sprouting roots. When it is established, transplant it into a bigger pot and keep it watered in a light, warm room. It will grow into a very attractive indoor plant.

Onion flowers ▲

You will need: one onion, toothpicks or sharpened wooden matchsticks and a small glass full of water.
Stick three toothpicks or sharpened matchsticks into the bottom of an onion and suspend it over a small glass of water so that only the lowest part of the onion is actually in the water. Leave it on a sunny window-sill and add water when necessary. The onion will soon sprout and send up pretty green leaves, eventually producing a flower.

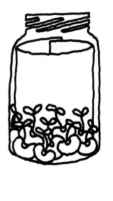

Vegetable top garden ●▲

You will need: the top of a root vegetable, a soup plate filled with water and a few pebbles.
Cut the tops of carrots, beets, turnips or parsnips, leaving only about a quarter inch of the vegetable still attached. Trim the leaves back until they are only about half an inch long and then stand the tops in a soup plate filled with water—the water should come about half-way up the vegetables. Keep the plate in a sunny place, water regularly and the vegetable leaves will grow quite tall within a couple of weeks.
To make this garden look prettier, line the bottom of the plate with pebbles and stand the vegetable tops in between them.

Jam-jar beans ●

You will need: an empty jam-jar, blotting paper, dried broad (lima) beans or lentils and some water.
Line the sides of an empty jam-jar with blotting-paper. Soak some dried broad [lima] beans or lentils in water for a few hours until they swell, then put them between the blotting-paper and the glass side of the jar. Pour about an inch of water into the jar—it will quickly soak up to the top of the blotting-paper. Keep the jar in a warm room and make sure there is always some water in the bottom of it. Within a day or two, the beans will start to grow shoots.

Mustard and cress garden ●

You will need: a large saucer, blotting paper and some mustard and cress.
If you don't have the patience to wait for weeks to watch a plant grow, mustard and cress is ideal because it starts sprouting within a few days of planting and thereafter you can almost see it grow. (Cress takes longer to start than mustard, so plant it first.)
Cover the bottom of a large saucer with two layers of blotting-paper, moisten it and sprinkle the cress seeds over it. Keep the saucer in a warm place and water it every day until the seeds start to sprout. Plant the mustard seeds in exactly the same way, three days after the cress.
The great excitement of this indoor gardening is that you can eat the end product!

Water gardens ■

You will need: A glass jar, water-glass, crystals of alum, iron sulphate and copper sulphate, silver sand and a knitting-needle or other long pointed implement.

A water garden is for growing chemicals not plants!

Most chemists and pharmacists sell the chemicals (don't let young children handle them) and aquarium shops sell the sand.

Fill the jar about three-quarters full with warm water, then add the water-glass and stir it in until the mixture is cold. Pour in the sand and let it sink to the bottom of the liquid until there is a layer of sand about one inch thick. Drop the crystals in, one by one, and press them under the sand with a knitting-needle or other long pointed implement. Leave the jar where it won't get knocked over or spilled and in a few days the crystals will 'grow' in strands of lovely colours.

 ## Moss gardens ■

You will need: a flat dish and some moss.

Moss dug up in small clumps outdoors —you will usually find it around trees in the park or in a forest—will grow indoors on a large flat dish. Fill the bottom of the dish with water before you put the moss in and thereafter water it once a week.

 ## Green-haired potatoes ●▲

You will need: a big potato, some absorbent cotton wool or blotting-paper, a small dish of water, some grass seeds and something to give the potato a face.

Scoop a hollow in the top of a big potato and slice off the bottom so that it will stand upright. Line the hollow with absorbent cotton wool or blotting-paper and stand the potato in a small dish of water. Sprinkle grass seed into the hollow and keep it watered, and within a few days the potato will sprout a fine head of green hair.

Give the potato eyes, ears and a nose with cloves, or anything that will stick into the potato, and you will have a growing potato head!

If you like you can substitute mustard and cress for the grass seed.

 ## Avocado plants ▲

You will need: the stone from a ripe avocado, a few toothpicks and a glass of water.

Avocado stones take a long time to start growing, but if you have patience they are worth the effort.

Wash the avocado stone in warm water and carefully peel away the dark brown skin, then stick enough toothpicks into it for it to stand, pointed end up, in a glass of water with two thirds of the stone above the surface. Keep it in a warm place away from direct light and add water when necessary.

In about six weeks the stone will split and a shoot will appear. When this happens you can move the stone into the light. When the stem is about six inches high, transplant it into a big flower pot, using good soil or potting compost. Water it twice a week.

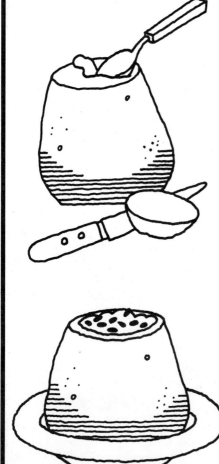

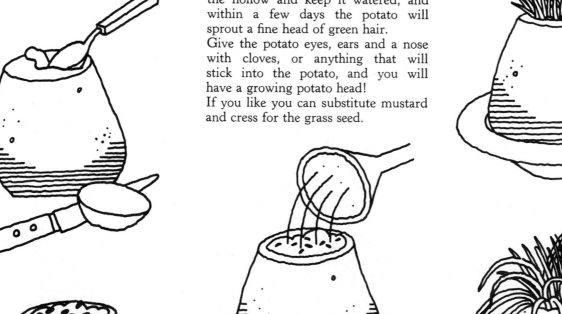

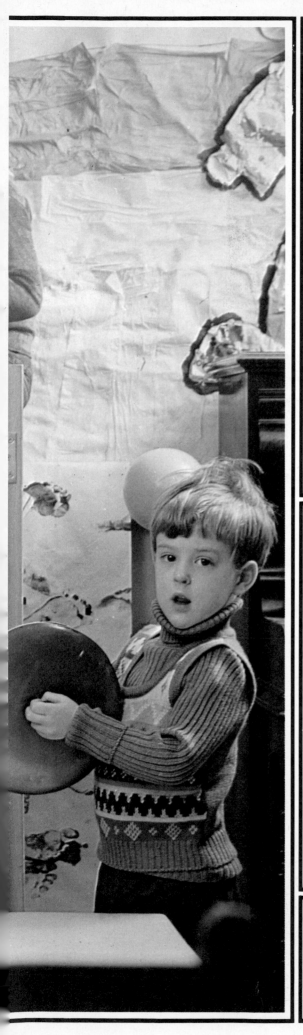

noisy things to do indoors

The suggestions in this section are not guaranteed to give you a splitting headache—but they well might. A game that one group of children play in deadly earnest and absolute silence may cause another group to riot—it depends largely on the children. So if any of these ideas produce a sepulchral calm you can count yourself lucky; if they produce the reverse, you have been warned!

One thing which is guaranteed to produce ear-splitting results is a band playing on home-made instruments. However, if you can stand it, the children will have a great time. The instruments can be collected and, in the case of the 'xylophone', made under parental supervision—which ones are made will, of course, depend upon what materials are available. You would be optimistic to expect the instruments to be made one day and played later—the children will want to use them immediately. So, explain how each one is played, help the 'band' to decide upon a tune everyone knows and then retire quickly to another room.

Instruments to hit. Drums can be made from almost any old cans or tough boxes, and wooden spoons are good drumsticks. Saucepan lids are satisfactory cymbals. To make a xylophone, fill empty glass bottles with different amounts of water and arrange them with the highest note at one end and the lowest at the other. Play it with a wooden spoon. Children playing the 'xylophone' should be supervised as the bottles could be knocked over—spilling water and, perhaps, breaking.

Instruments to shake. Rice or dried peas in an empty washing-up liquid bottle, or a can with a tight lid, will make good maraccas for a calypso beat. Two metal spoons clack together like castanets (well, almost).

Instruments to pluck. A harp or guitar can be made by stretching rubber bands across an empty shoe-box or similar small cardboard container.

Instruments to blow. The easiest is a piece of tissue paper wrapped round a comb. More complicated is a fife made from a cardboard tube. To make this cover one end of the tube with waxed paper and punch five small holes in row along the tube. The tube will amplify any sound hummed into it.

This 'band' of children (left) are playing a variety of home-made instruments including saucepan lid cymbals, a xylophone, tin can maraccas, a paper megaphone trumpet and rattling instruments—bells and bottle-tops attached to sticks.

Paper battle ▲

You will need: old newspapers and cardboard boxes.

Crumple up sheets of newspaper into 'cannon balls', divide into two teams and let each side construct its own 'castle' from the furniture in the room or from old cardboard boxes. Each team stays behind its own defences and 'fires' on the enemy. There are no winners or losers in this battle, but everyone has a good time.

Scarecrow's hat ▲

You will need: a broomstick, some string, an old hat and some newspapers.

Tie a broomstick to the back of a chair and balance an old hat on the top. Use balls of crumpled-up newspaper to try to knock the scarecrow's hat off.

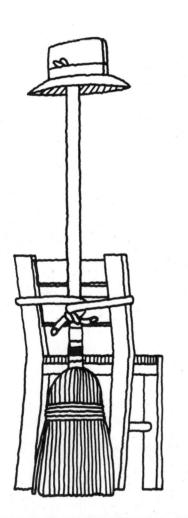

Bowling alley ■

You will need: a cardboard box, scissors, cardboard, sticky tape, crayons or a pencil and some marbles or other small balls.

Cut some arches into the top side of an old cardboard box and stand it upside down on the floor. The arches should be just big enough to accommodate whatever 'bowls' you can find—marbles, tennis balls, etc. If you are going to keep a score, number the arches and make them different sizes—low numbers for wide arches and high numbers for narrower ones.

If there are arguments about which arch the bowls went through, you may have to make little lanes behind each arch. Cut strips of cardboard and stick them into place with sticky tape or glue so that the bowls can't escape, and there can be no disagreement.

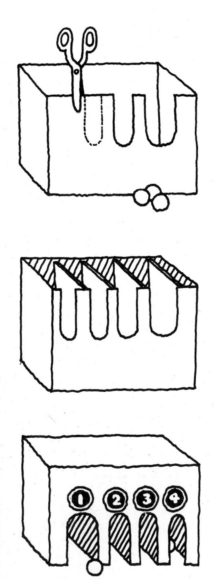

Match-box radio ■

You will need: a length of thin string, two match-boxes and scissors.

This is good fun for older children with enough imagination to make up their own stories.

Make a hole through both sides of one match-box and only one side of another. Thread a piece of thin string about 30 inches long through the match-box with one hole and knot it inside. This end will be the ear-phone. Thread the other end of the string right through the other match-box and knot it. This will be the transmitter.

One child holds the 'ear-phone' match-box against his ear while another tells a story, pulls the string tight and makes suitable sound effects at the transmitting end to go with his story. The variations are astonishing: by rotating the string in the hole or scratching the transmitting match-box you can make applause or sawing noises or machine-gun fire. Any number of extraordinary sounds can be produced by experiment.

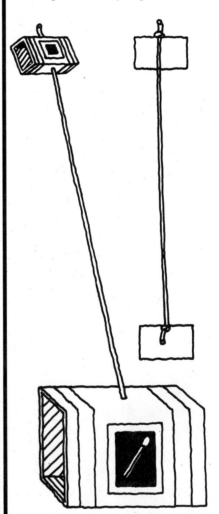

Catch-ball ▲

You will need: a thick sheet of paper, some thin paper, glue or sticky tape and a piece of thread or wool.

Roll a thick sheet of paper into a cone and stick it with glue or sticky tape. Crumple a couple of sheets of paper into a tight, small ball and tie a piece of thread or wool around it. Stick the other end of the thread into the inside of the cone. Toss the ball into the air and see how many times you can catch it in the cone.

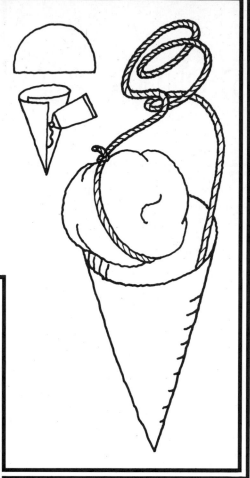

Throw-a-number ■

You will need: some rubber or cardboard rings, a large sheet of paper and a pencil and ruler.

Collect together some rubber rings from preserving jars, or some small table mats or beer mats. (If you can't find anything to use as ready-made throwing discs, make some by cutting out circles of thick cardboard.) Mark up a large sheet of white or brown paper into squares slightly bigger than your throwing discs and number each square. The idea is to throw the discs on to the paper to see how much you can score—each disc has to be completely within a square to score. (It is more difficult to get a disc in the square on the outside of the sheet, so these should score higher than squares in the centre.)

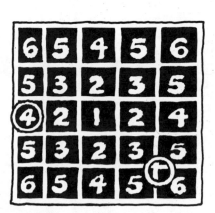

Pot-ball ▲

You will need: some empty yogurt or cottage cheese cartons, crayons, paper and marbles or old buttons.

This is a good game for two or three children—but you need to be able to add up.

Decorate and number as many empty yogurt or cottage cheese cartons as you can, stand them on the floor in a line, the higher numbers being progressively further away, and see how many marbles you can throw into them from a reasonable distance. (If you haven't got any marbles, use old buttons or small balls made of crumpled paper.)

You score according to the number on the outside of the carton—one point for carton number one which is nearest to you, six points for carton number six as it is further away and so more difficult to get a marble into.

(Smaller children can play this without scoring, just trying to get the marbles into the containers.)

Aunt Sally ●

You will need: a few small cardboard packets, paint, a knotted handkerchief, and a table top you can use.

Paint faces on a few small cardboard packets then line them up on a table top. Stand a good distance away and then see how many packets you can knock down by throwing a knotted handkerchief at them—having first, of course, made sure that there is nothing valuable around that you might knock over.

make believe

Bird

Bull

Children of all ages love make-believe games, from simple dressing-up to creating elaborate adventures in an atomic submarine that may appear to be no more than a box in the garage to an adult. By 'making-believe' children develop their imagination, increase the scope of their play and live out their fantasies. (It is a world to which many an adult would like occasionally to return.)

Although most children are happy to develop their own make-believe games (and sometimes resent the intrusion of adults), they can be helped by being provided with some basic raw materials and given the occasional pointer. A very young child, for example, may not see the potential in an old sheet, but when an adult points out that a strip torn off it would make a very good pretend bandage, whole new worlds of possibility open up for endless games of doctors and hospitals and nurses. And a child, if encouraged, can transform the most mundane piece of furniture—a row of chairs becomes a Jumbo jet flying the Atlantic, a bed is a canoe negotiating terrible rapids, a blanket thrown over a table is a tent pitched on the side of Everest, and so on.

The point of dressing-up is for children to pretend they are what they are not—they are therefore almost certain to act the role of a grown-up or a baby. A box of discarded adult clothes, particularly hats, shoes, skirts and old jewellery, can give children hours and hours of entertainment—and if you can get together bits and pieces of old uniforms their bliss will be complete. If no real clothes are available, plenty of fun can be had by making clothes from old newspapers—it is not the cleanest game in the world, but then the best games never are. Skirts can be made by wrapping the newspaper round a child's waist and tucking it into a belt, and tunic tops are easily created by tearing a hole out of the middle of a big sheet of newspaper and slipping it over the head.

Demands for fancy dress can impose a considerable strain on an adult's imagination, let alone that of children. The most popular and easy fancy dress outfits are: pirates—curtain rings for ear-rings, cardboard eye-patches, scarf over the head and so on; gypsies—long skirts, apron, ear-rings, blouse, scarf and shawl; tramps—ragged old clothes and shoes, suitably dirtied, bundle tied in cotton scarf on the end of a stick, and clowns—baggy pyjama trousers, smock, funny make-up.

Shadow theatre

You will need: a white sheet and a strong lamp and, if you want to use cut-out characters, cardboard, scissors and wire.

The actors can be live or little cardboard cut-outs—the principle is exactly the same; only the scale is different. To stage a shadow theatre show in real life, hang a white sheet across a room in front of a strong lamp. Turn off all the other lights in the room. The actors must play their parts between the sheet and the single light so that their shadows fall on to the sheet where they can be seen by the audience on the other side.

(Children who might ordinarily be a little inhibited by putting on a show can cope much more easily with a shadow play because the sheet gives them security from the reactions of the audience.)

On a smaller scale it can be just as much fun to stage a shadow play using simple cut-out figures held by short pieces of wire, or an animal story using your hands to make the animal heads.

You can make all sorts of shadow people and animals just by using your hands. Here are a few of them.

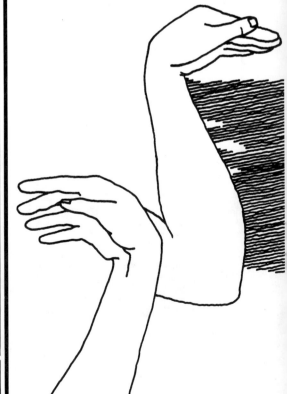

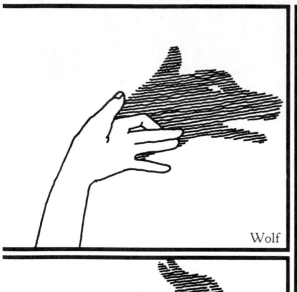

Wolf

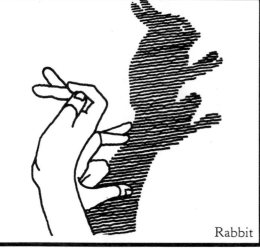

Rabbit

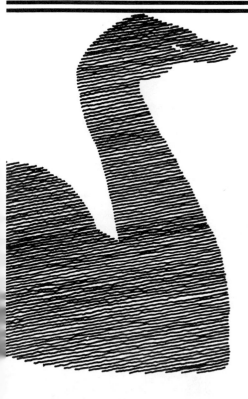

Swan

Hats ▲

You will need: thin cardboard, scissors crayons, glue and, if you have them, gold, silver or coloured paper, sequins and feathers.

To make a crown, cut a strip of thin cardboard about 4 inches wide and 24 inches long. If you can find some gold or silver paper, glue it on to the cardboard then cut a zig-zag pattern along one edge. Paste on coloured-paper, jewels or sequins, then measure it around your head and stick the ends together.

A wizard's or a clown's hat can be made by folding a sheet of thick paper into the shape of a cone and glueing the sides together. Cut the bottom off so that it is straight and decorate the hat with magic signs for a wizard and big spots for a clown.

An American Indian's head-dress is easy to make if you can find some feathers. Cut two thin strips of paper and glue the feathers in between them. Measure the paper strip round your head and glue the ends together so that it fits.

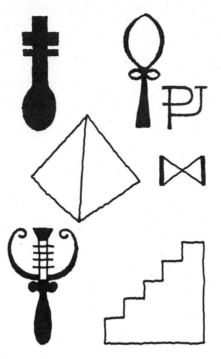

You could trace these ancient good luck signs (above) and transfer them on to a wizard's hat. And, from left to right, there are pictures of two steps in making a crown, two in a wizard's hat, four in an American Indian's head-dress, two in paper plate masks and, far right, two stages in making a paper bag mask.

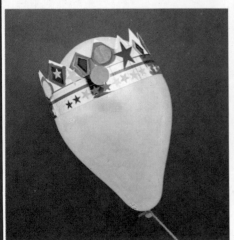

Masks ▲

You will need: thin cardboard, scissors, elastic, crayons, paper bags, paper plates, paint and oddments of wool.

For the kind of mask you would wear to a ball, fold a piece of thin cardboard in half and draw the outline of half the mask on one side, using the folded edge as the centre. Cut around the outline, through both pieces of the cardboard and the mask will be symmetrical. Carefully cut out the eye holes and punch two small holes on each side to hold a piece of hat elastic. Simpler masks—and ones with a lot more play potential—can be made from big paper bags. Cut holes for eyes and mouth and then paint any kind of face— animal, monster, dragon, witch, clown —on to the bag. Paper ears and woollen 'hair' can be glued-on if you like. For the sort of mask that just covers the face, a paper plate is about the right size and shape. Cut the eyes and mouth out first, then paint on the face. Make small holes on each side at eye level and tie on elastic, or add a cardboard strap to hold it on.

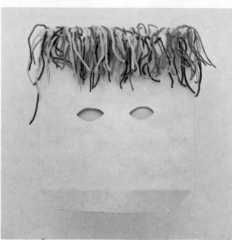

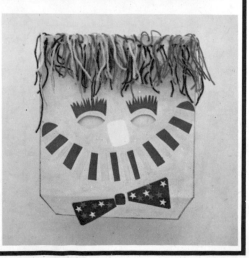

messy things to do indoors

Children, particularly young children, seem to prefer messy games. Hand and foot printing, for example, is always a bigger favourite than colouring or drawing with crayons.

Children simply enjoy covering themselves with water or paint—this is why face painting is always popular.

Theatrical grease paint is the best stuff to use for face painting because it is harmless to the skin, comes in many different colours and can be removed with cream. The problems are that it is expensive and not easily available. Old lipsticks will probably make a satisfactory substitute for most children and they won't worry that there is not much colour variation— the sheer enjoyment of making a mess of their faces is usually sufficient. Do not encourage face painting with an ordinary box of paints or felt tipped pens—the designs may not come off and could irritate sensitive skins.

If possible, of course, it is best to let children play outdoors with water in warm weather—then they don't get cold and you don't have to clear up puddles in the house. If, however, this is impossible games centred around the bath or strategically placed bowls of water will keep children amused and should not cause too much havoc. But it is sensible to protect the players and their immediate environment with plastic aprons, newspapers and whatever else is handy. And remember that very young children should never be allowed to play with water unaccompanied.

Water play can be instructive, too. The best boats, for example, are those made by the children themselves, using their own imagination. (See No. 80). It is certainly worth letting them find out which things will float and which won't, how to use weight to make the boat more stable and how to fix the sail so that if you blow it will go forward through the water. Clearly the older the child the more he or she will appreciate the processes involved.

Another popular messy thing is playing with clay.

Between the ages of two and three, children seldom have any interest in clay modelling beyond thumping it, tearing it apart, sticking it back together and moulding different shapes with their hands. Clay suitable for this can be made in the kitchen with the following ingredients: 1 cup salt, 1½ cups flour, ½ cup water, 2 tablespoons oil. Mix them all into a dough and add a couple of drops of food colouring if you want to make it more interesting visually. This 'clay' will last for weeks if it is kept in a plastic bag or covered jar in a refrigerator, and any particularly well-loved models will harden if left uncovered.

Older children may like to use this home-made clay for more advanced modelling, but when it dries it becomes very brittle and breaks easily—which is upsetting for a child who has spent a lot of time and trouble on a particular model.

There are dozens of modelling materials now available which harden into a stone-like finish and which can be painted. Pottery clay, available from most art shops, is a good, cheap modelling material which will last indefinitely if kept in a crock with a lid. Wrap it in a damp cloth before you put it away and it will stay soft and malleable.

Most children don't need any instructions on what to make or how to make it—they are best left to work it out for themselves. One hint that might be worth passing on, however, is the best way of joining two pieces of pottery clay. They will stick together with simple pressure but the join will always be liable to break when it hardens. The best way of solving this difficulty is to make up a kind of glue, called 'slip', by taking a dollop of clay and mixing it in a cup with water until it is the consistency of cream. If this is smeared on to both sides that need to be joined, it will cement them firmly together.

Hand and foot printing

You will need: a large sheet of paper and paints.

This is a simple, thoroughly enjoyable form of printing for young children. All you have to do is paint the palm of one hand or the sole of one foot— or both—and press them on to a large sheet of paper. The result is very satisfactory and good patterns can be formed by printing a number of hands and feet in different colours. The best paint to use is the powder variety, mixed fairly thickly, and it is not, of course, a good idea to use any kind of paint that won't wash off reasonably easily.

Finger painting

You will need: a large sheet of paper, flour and water, poster paint, old bowls, stiff cardboard, scissors and old combs or forks.

Small children love this tactile and incredibly messy experience. Remember to protect everything in sight before they begin!

Mix flour and water paste with poster paint until it forms a thick cream and pour three or four different colours into separate bowls. Spread out a large sheet of paper, dip your fingers into the paint and draw on the paper with them. Old combs and forks as well as fingers can be used and make interesting patterns when pulled through the paint. A piece of stiff cardboard with one edge cut in a zig-zag works very well, too.

Dribble pictures

You will need: paints and a piece of paper.

Drop a dollop of paint in the centre of a piece of paper, then hold the paper up and let the paint run downwards. Keep turning the paper to stop the paint dripping off the edge. Repeat with as many more colours as you like.

Block printing

You will need: a root vegetable, knife, paints, paint brush, paper napkins, shallow trays and a large sheet of paper.

Large sheets printed in repeating patterns in different colours can look very effective and they are useful for wrapping presents or covering books. (Younger children may not be able to keep making one firm imprint in the correct position, but even if they do nothing but drag the block backwards and forwards over the paper they will still be having fun.)

The first thing to do is to make the block. You can use a potato or carrot. Slice the vegetable in half and cut out a pattern on the flat side. (Remember the pattern will be printed from what is left, not what is cut away.)

If carving a vegetable block proves difficult, remember that very effective prints can be made simply by using half a cucumber, green pepper or almost any seed vegetable.

To start printing, either pour the paint into shallow trays lined with paper napkins so that they make pads of different colours, or simply paint the printing side of the block with a thick paintbrush.

Experiment first on an old piece of paper both to make sure that the block is printing satisfactorily and to practise pressing it down firmly and squarely. Then take a large sheet of paper and start printing.

Leaf printing

You will need: a leaf, paper, a soft wax crayon, carbon paper and an old newspaper.

The simplest way of taking a leaf print is to lay the leaf on a flat surface with the veins upwards, cover it with a sheet of white paper and rub over it very lightly with a soft wax crayon.

Better prints can be taken with carbon paper, but you must first press the leaf between newspaper for 24 hours to absorb any moisture. Then lay it face down on a newspaper, cover it with the carbon paper, also face down, and cover that with three or four sheets of newspaper. Using your finger-nails, rub all over the area of the leaf so that it is coated by carbon. Take off the covering sheets of newspaper and carbon paper and place the leaf, face upwards, on to a sheet of white paper. Be careful not to move it or the print will smudge. Cover it with a single sheet of newspaper and rub very gently with your fingernail once more. Lift off the leaf and it will leave a perfect white outline shape.

Double pictures

You will need: paints, a paint brush and paper.

Fold a sheet of paper in half, then open it out again. Quickly paint a picture on one side of the paper and while the paint is still wet, fold it up again and press hard. When it is opened out, the picture will have doubled.

Drip pictures

You will need: paper and paints.

Drip dots of different coloured paint all over a sheet of paper, then blow gently in different directions to make the colours run and mix with each other.

Tie-dye

You will need: a T-shirt or other garment you wish to dye, a packet of cold-water dye, a bucket, some old buttons, dried peas and thin, strong string.

T-shirts and handkerchiefs are the best things to tie-dye. Put a big button under the centre of the T-shirt or handkerchief, wrap the fabric over it and tie it tightly underneath so that the button is encased in the fabric. Use up the rest of the material by tying in peas and buttons in whatever positions you like. It is very important to tie the string as tightly as possible underneath each pea and button.

Mix up the cold-water dye according to the instructions on the packet, drop in your T-shirt or handkerchief and leave it for about 30 minutes. When you take it out, rinse it thoroughly under the cold water tap, then unfasten all the wrappings. Where the string has been tied the dye is unable to penetrate the fabric, so you should be left with a nice pattern of white circles all over it.

Wax scratching

You will need: a sheet of thick paper, wax crayons and a toothpick or old fork.

Using wax crayons, cover an entire sheet of thick paper with patches of different colours, then cover the whole pattern with a black crayon. You can now scratch a pattern on to the paper with a toothpick or the prongs of a fork. Gently scrape away the black wax so that the colours underneath shine through.

Papier mâché I

You will need: old newspapers, a bucket, water, wallpaper paste.

Most children enjoy making papier mâché even if they don't particularly want to use the result.

First you need to tear up the old newspapers into small pieces. Drop them into a bucket and pour water over them so that they become soaked. Drain the water away and squeeze down the paper pulp to get as much excess water out as possible. Then sprinkle a cupful of wallpaper paste into the bucket and mix it in with your fingers until all the paper has a coating of glue. Add more water if necessary or more paste if it doesn't feel sticky enough. When it is a thick, mushy pulp, the papier mâché can be modelled like plasticine or clay to make puppets' heads, dolls or bowls.

Papier mâché II

You will need: old newspapers, a mould, petroleum jelly, wallpaper paste, scissors and paint.

This more sophisticated version of papier mâché, suitable for older children, builds the paper layer on layer. You need a mould of some sort—a vase, plate or bowl. Cover this well with vaseline petroleum jelly. Then stick newspaper scraps about one inch square on to the mould; the vaseline will hold them. Next mix up some wallpaper paste and coat the newspaper layer all over. Before the paste dries stick another layer of newspaper on. Continue pasting and papering until you have at least 8 layers of paper.

It is best to leave papier mâché to dry for a couple of days before removing the mould and painting it. If you can leave it near a radiator or in a warm place it will dry more quickly.

Almost anything can be used as a mould for a papier mâché model, provided it does not narrow at the top, (which would make it impossible to take the papier mâché off), and it is first smeared with grease to avoid the papier mâché sticking. The lower half of a bottle is a good mould for a papier mâché pencil holder, for example. Smear grease on the bottle and cover the bottom and

sides with an even layer of papier mâché. When it has dried hard, ease the bottle out, trim the rim of the holder with scissors, then paint it.

A good method of making a large, round, hollow ball of papier mâché is to blow up a balloon, smear it lightly with vaseline or grease of some kind, then cover it with layers of papier mâché. Leave the knot of the balloon uncovered and when the papier mâché is dry, burst the balloon and pull it clear.

This basic shape, with suitable additions, can be used to make an owl, a fat piggy, a Father Christmas or the face of a very fat man or woman.

Sculptures

You will need: newspaper, a knife and a block of salt or a large tablet of soap. Carving a model out of a solid block is a satisfying method of creating, but far from the easiest. Young children probably won't get much satisfaction from this method simply because they will get frustrated by lack of achievement. But from the age of six onwards carving simple models begins to be a possibility.

The simplest material to carve is a block of salt, sometimes called a loaf. Spread out a newspaper and put the salt block on it, then with a blunt knife or spoon cut and scrape away at the block to make your sculpture. (Keep the scraped off salt for the kitchen.) If it is an animal, have him sitting or lying down because legs often get too thin and crumble away. Ships are good things to carve out of salt blocks.

Soap carving is easy, too, and has the added satisfaction of being definitely useful—the carved bar being used as your personal bath soap. (And you can keep the scraped off soap to put in your bath mitt if you have one.)

Boats
●▲

You will need: polystyrene dishes, plasticine or modelling clay, pencils or lollipop sticks, paper and scissors.

The dishes used in supermarkets as trays for meat and fruit are good starting points for a boat. A blob of plasticine or modelling clay put in the middle of a dish will weight and balance the boat and hold a mast made from a pencil or lollipop stick and any piece of paper will do for the sail.

Trays from match-boxes will also float satisfactorily, although some types won't last more than half an hour without disintegrating.

To make the balance problem more interesting use your boat to transport lead animals or soldiers across a 'sea' or 'river'—if you put them all in one end you will find the boat sinks!

See-through painting
■

You will need: a wooden frame, a sheet of polythene, sticky tape and paints and brushes.

Stretch the polythene over the frame and hold it in place with sticky tape. Prop it up in a light position either indoors or out. Then just paint on to the polythene what you see through it. For life-like results mix your paints to match the colours you see.

Spatter prints
▲

You will need: an old tooth-brush, a palette knife, thinly mixed poster paints, a leaf, some pins and paper.

This is a pretty way of making outline shapes.

Pin whatever it is you are going to outline—a leaf is a good thing to start with—to a sheet of paper. Dip the tooth-brush into the paint, then holding the brush downwards over the paper, scrape the bristles towards you with the knife. The paint will spatter on to the paper in tiny dots. When it is dry, lift off the leaf and it will leave a perfect white outline shape.

Carved panels
■

You will need: a shallow tin lid, round or square, with straight edges, grease, plaster of Paris, water, a soft pencil, a knife, a skewer and poster paints.

Mix the plaster of Paris with water in a bowl until it is a thick paste. Grease the inside of the tin lid, then pour in the paste until the lid is filled. Smooth the top if necessary, then let it set hard overnight.

Use a blunt knife and the point of a skewer as carving tools. It helps to draw a design on the plaster with a soft pencil before you start. Any kind of picture can be carved—simple flowers, ships, faces and heraldic shields all look good. Use poster paint to colour the panel when the carving is finished, then ease the panel out of the tin lid.

Fishing
▲

You will need: plastic cartons with lids, crayons, plasticine or modelling clay, hair pins or paper-clips, string and a long stick.

First you need fish! Make them from plastic cartons with lids, empty plastic bottles tightly stoppered or waxed cardboard packages. Colour them with crayons, then stick a small lump of plasticine or modelling clay inside each container and replace the top or stopper. This weight will keep the fish floating upright.

Put the fish in the water and look to see which part floats highest in the water. Fix a loop at this point made from a hairpin, paper-clip (or piece of thick fuse-wire).

To make your fishing rod, tie a hook made from a hairpin or paper-clip on to one end of a piece of string and tie the other end to a long stick or ruler.

With your fish swimming happily in the bath or bowl you are ready to start fishing. You can make it into a game to play with other children by numbering the fish and keeping a score.

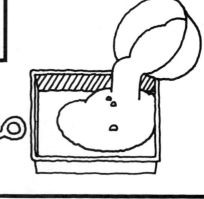

Spatter prints (right) and see-through painting (inset) are fun to do and keep.

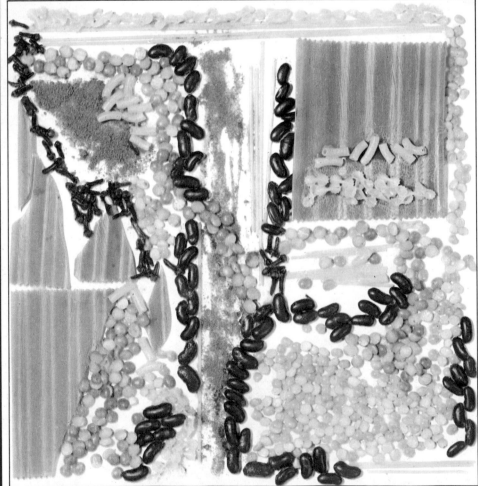

collages

A collage is an artistic composition in three dimensions, usually either glued or sewn together. One of the nicest things about making collages is that almost anything can be used, scraps of fabric, dry foods, egg-shells, even twigs and leaves.

Four ways with collage—a fabric one (above);
one made from treasured oddments (centre);
a see-what-happens collage
using foods from the kitchen (bottom left),
and (top left) a paper collage by the famous artist, Matisse.

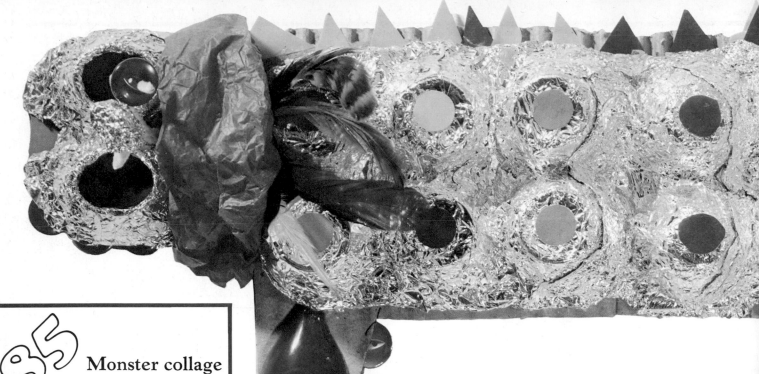

Monster collage ■

You will need: a large sheet of cardboard, a pencil, glue, egg-boxes, silver paper and other odds and ends.

A wicked-looking monster can be made very realistically in the form of a collage. Find a really big sheet of cardboard and draw the outline of the monster. Then look for things to fill in the outline with—cones of egg-boxes for his bumpy body and big balls of screwed-up silver foil for his eyes and tongue. Use your imagination to make him the most fearful monster in the world.

A living picture ■

You will need: a large picture of the countryside, cardboard, glue, absorbent cotton wool, twigs, salt and anything else that will make your picture 'come alive'.

Take a big picture of a countryside scene, look at it carefully and see how much of it you can bring to life.

Salt makes convincing snow, little twigs can become trees, fine sand will make a beach, tufts of absorbent cotton wool can be clouds, and so on.

Stick the picture on to a piece of cardboard, then look around for what you can stick onto it. Paste over each area carefully and glue on your real-life additions. You may not be able to finish the picture immediately, but once you have started it you will know what you are looking for.

Paper collage ●

You will need: a large sheet of stiff paper, glue and as many other different kinds of paper as possible.

Collect together as many different kinds of paper as you can find, looking particularly for lots of different colours, thicknesses and textures. Even shiny foil and sweet wrappings should be included. Cut or tear the papers into whatever shapes you want and stick them, piece by piece, on to a large sheet of stiff paper. You can make a pattern that pleases you, or you can stick them into a shape like a windmill or a bird—but if you do this it is easier if you draw the shape first.

Wool collage ▲

You will need: a large sheet of white cardboard, a pencil, glue and scraps of wool.

Draw a big, simple flower on to a sheet of white cardboard. Collect together as many scraps of wool as you can find. Then, working on a small part of the flower at a time, fill in the petals, leaves and stalk by glueing on lengths of wool cut to the right size. For the centre of the flower, stick the wool down in a spiral.

Fluffy duckling ●

You will need: yellow tissue paper, pencil, glue, stiff white paper, scissors, paint and cardboard.

Tear the tissue paper into little pieces and roll up all the pieces into tiny round balls. Draw the outline of a duckling on a piece of stiff white paper, then paste it with glue and stick on the balls of tissue paper as close together as possible. Cut his legs, beak and eyes out of cardboard, paint them and stick them into position.

Fabric collage

91 ▲

You will need: a thin sheet of cardboard, scraps of fabric, scissors and glue or a needle and cotton.
A fabric collage looks best if it is sewn together, but if you can't sew you can stick the pieces down. Glue a piece of plain-coloured fabric on to a thin sheet of cardboard, then cut up the fabric scraps and arrange them in a pattern or in a picture. Glue them or sew them into position, piece by piece.

Spaghetti collage

93 ●▲

You will need: brown paper, spaghetti and drawing pins [thumb tacks].
Pin a large piece of brown paper on a wall. Get an adult to cook some spaghetti until it is almost, but not quite, cooked. Let it cool just enough so that you don't burn your fingers when you touch it, then just throw it strand by strand at the brown paper. It will stick on in all sorts of interesting squiggly patterns. (If it is completely cooked it will not stick.)
Leave the spaghetti picture to cool and harden—it will keep for a long time.

See-what-happens collage

92 ●▲■

You will need: a piece of cardboard, a pot of glue and four or five cups of almost any dry, loose material from the kitchen cupboard—rice, breakfast cereal, split peas, macaroni, sugar, and so on.
Pour a small amount of glue on to the cardboard in any shape that you like—wiggly lines, blobs, anything at all. Then shake on to the cardboard the contents of one cup. Let it settle on to the glue for a few moments, then lift the cardboard and brush away the surplus that has not stuck.
Repeat the process with more glue and more material until you are satisfied with the picture. When the glue has dried, you can paint the collage if you wish, or leave it with its natural colours.

Egg-shell collage

90 ▲

You will need: six empty egg-shells, pencil, thick paper, glue and some paint.
Clean the egg-shells and break them into small pieces. Draw an animal shape on a piece of thick paper or thin cardboard—an animal with a scaly coat is most suitable, something like a crocodile or a dragon. Paste all over the inside of the shape, then, piece by piece, stick on the egg-shells to make his coat. When it is dry, paint on his eyes and a red tongue. There is no need to paint the rest of the egg-shells unless you want to.

Autumn leaf picture

94 ■

You will need: leaves, white paper, crayons or paint and glue.
The glorious red and gold autumn leaves can make a really attractive indoor picture. Collect as many different leaves as you can find in as many different shades as possible. On a large sheet of white paper draw the trunk and branches of a tree and paint or crayon it in dark brown. When the paint is dry, stick the leaves on to the branches with glue.

All children have to suffer the excruciating boredom of spending some time in bed getting over mumps, chicken-pox, measles or whatever. When the illness is at its height they will probably be content to lie in bed and do nothing, but the moment they start to feel better their natural energy is going to need an outlet. It is a difficult time for everyone—the child is bored with being made to stay in bed and the parents are probably beginning to feel the strain of running up and down stairs to cater to the demands of a fractious and reluctant invalid. The next pages contain suggestions on how to keep the child amused and so alleviate the problem to some extent. Give the child a large tray to keep all bits and pieces on; this reduces the amount of mess involved.

The section on quiet things to do indoors (Nos. 1-36) also includes games and suggestions of things to make which are suitable for a child who has to stay in bed.

Younger children may not want to bother with the business of learning a game or concentrating on some task when they are feeling ill. The ideal solution for them is a tray or cardboard box full of bits and pieces which they can do what they like with. Spring clothes-pegs and wooden matches, a magnet and a pile of paper-clips, a padlock and key, a magnifying-glass, an old clock which can be taken to pieces—all of these are the kind of 'toys' liable to fascinate young children.

95 Alphabet doodling ▲

You will need: paper and crayons. Write some capital letters on to a clean sheet of paper and see what pictures you can turn them into.

Making an alphabet book (left) is a very good way of passing the time when you have to stay in bed after an illness.

96 Clock patience ▲

You will need: a large sheet of cardboard, a pencil and a pack of cards. This is an easy card game for children of four years old and upwards provided that they don't mind if they don't always win.

Draw a clock face on the large sheet of cardboard. Number it normally except for making 11 and 12 Jack and Queen, and in the centre of the clock draw in the King. Deal out a pack of cards face down round the clock so that each 'hour', and the centre, has four cards. Take the top card from the centre pile, look at it and put it, face upwards, on the bottom of the pile of that number. Then take the top card from that pile and continue in the same way. The object is to sort the cards into their appropriate numbers around the clock before all the Kings arrive in the middle. As soon as the four Kings are exposed the game is ended as you have no card to pick up and you must start again at the beginning.

Finger puppets ▲

You will need: crayons and, if you have them, thimbles, match-boxes, wool, a brush and paste.

These are good companions in bed and are easy to make.

The simplest way is to draw a face on the tip of one finger. Thimbles make good hats, and you can make moustaches and hair from strands of wool and stick them on with paste.

If you draw faces on two fingers and stick them up through the wrapper of a match-box you can make them have conversations.

If you don't want to make the end of your fingers messy, you can make a head from plasticine or modelling clay and make a hole in the bottom of it so that you can put the head on your finger.

Hand faces ●

You will need: crayons.

Look at the way the creases in the palm of your hand move as you open and close your fingers. Then draw a face on your palm using the creases to form expressions. If, for example, you draw an eye underneath your first finger (forefinger), you will find that your 'face' will wink very effectively when you waggle your finger.

Face puzzle ●

You will need: a small tray—the kind that supermarkets use for packaging fruit and meat—crayons, two buttons and a piece of cellophane if you have it.

Draw a face on the tray—but leave out the eyes. Put the two buttons in the tray and then slide it around to see if you can get the buttons into position as the eyes.

If you cover the tray with a piece of cellophane (or a large clear plastic bag) and stick it underneath, you will be able to shake the tray as well as sliding it.

Mobiles ▲■

You will need: pipe-cleaners or wire cut into lengths, cotton thread or string and cardboard.

These are good things to make in bed and give a lot of pleasure to a child who, for a lot of the day, simply wants something to look at. They can be as complex or as simple as the child likes.

For an easy mobile take two pipe-cleaners or lengths of wire and twist them together at the centre. Cut out four cardboard shapes—any shape you like but they should all be more or less the same size or the mobile will not be balanced. Make a hole through each piece of cardboard and tie a piece of thread through it, then tie the other end of the thread to the end of one of the wire 'arms'. Tie on the other three cardboard shapes in the same way. Finally, tie a long piece of thread to the centre of the mobile—where the wire arms are twisted together—and use the other end to attach your mobile to the ceiling or hang it in an open window. (Get someone else to do this for you.)

You can, of course, make more complicated mobiles which have more than four arms, or colour the cardboard before you tie it on. But don't make them too large or else you won't be able to feel them for balance by holding them over the side of your bed.

Invisible writing ■

You will need: paper, a pen with a nib and the juice of a lemon.

This is a good way of sending secret messages to your friends—providing that they know how to make the message appear!

Make sure the pen-nib is clean and using the lemon juice as 'ink' write your message. It will disappear as it dries.

To make the message re-appear, just warm the paper over an electric light bulb or a radiator.

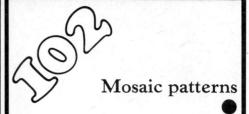

Mosaic patterns ●

You will need: different coloured papers, scissors, cardboard and glue.

Cut the coloured pieces of paper into little squares (or any shape you want). Then glue them on to a piece of stiff cardboard to make a picture or a pattern.

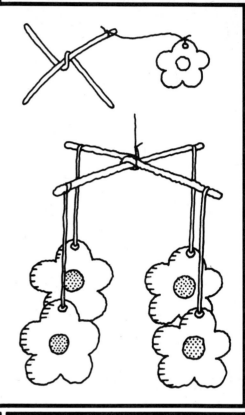

Draught-board puzzle ■

You will need: a sheet of paper, a pencil and eight counters.

This is a difficult puzzle to solve but it provides a real challenge to a child.

Divide a sheet of paper into 64 squares—the same as a draught-board. (Obviously, if you have a draught-board, use it.) Then take eight counters or draughts and place them so that no more than one counter is on any line, either from top to bottom, side to side, or corner to corner (diagonally). (See solution page.)

Tangram ▲■

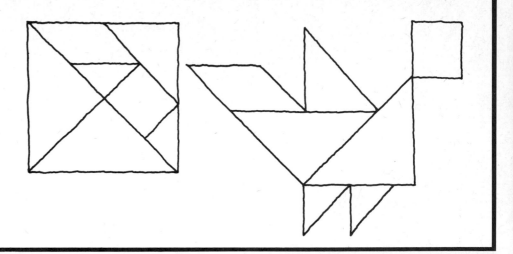

You will need: tracing paper, a sheet of white paper, crayons and scissors. Trace this pattern exactly on to a square of white paper. Colour the different sections, then cut them up. You can use a tangram as a jigsaw, putting the pieces back together to form a square, or make 'pictures' by using the shapes in different ways.

Embroidered dishcloth ■

You will need: a printed dishcloth with a bold pattern, embroidery silks, scissors and needles.

This is a good thing for an older child to do and has the added advantage that whatever stage it is left in it looks finished.

Look at the pattern or picture on the dishcloth and see how you can improve it with embroidery—simple stitches will do. You could outline the edge of the dishcloth with a daisy stitch or cross stitch or completely fill in part of the pattern with satin stitch.

Paper beads ▲

You will need: sheets of coloured paper or wallpaper (not too thick), scissors, a brush, paste, a knitting-needle, paints and string.
Cut the paper into narrow strips about 12 inches long and a quarter of an inch wide. Paste the strips on the plain side of the paper and roll them around the knitting-needle. You will find it is possible to make all kinds of different shapes by rolling the paper in different ways. Slide each bead off the needle and put it somewhere to dry. Then paint the beads and thread them on to string to make into jewellery.

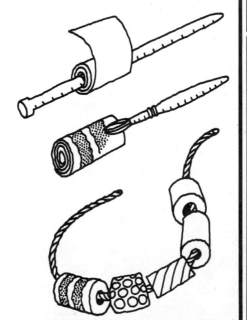

Animated pin people ▲■

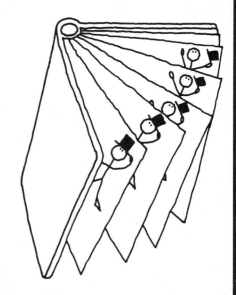

You will need: an old book that you can draw in and some crayons.
Start with a right-hand page, then on every other page (i.e. every right-hand page) draw a little pin man or woman in the top right-hand margin. Draw your pin person with a slight movement on each successive page. If you do all this reasonably carefully, then when you flick the corners of the book the man will leap into action. He can dance, put on or take off a hat, fight with another man or perform just about any kind of acrobatics.
(Animated cartoons—like early Walt Disney ones—are drawn step by step like this.)

Alphabet book ●

You will need: a large exercise book or drawing book, old magazines, scissors, a brush and a pot of paste.
Draw the letters of the alphabet on successive pages in the exercise book. Then look through the magazines and cut out as many pictures as possible of objects beginning with different letters and stick them into the book on the appropriate pages.

party games

The best children's parties are those that are highly organized, but appear not to be. Most children like plenty of action at a party and the games likely to prove most popular are those that involve everyone rushing about. That is fine, but you must have some quieter games ready for when the guests need a breathing space—just after they have eaten for example.

Children love the well-tried, well-known games that are familiar to them all. They enjoy learning the occasional new game but there is no point in dreaming up a continuous programme of new games that none of the guests has ever heard of. Pass the Parcel, Musical Chairs, Hunt the Slipper and Squeak, Piggy, Squeak are the kinds of games that have been enjoyed by generations of children and there is no reason to think that they will not continue to be enjoyed for generations to come.

For a good children's party decide in advance which games are going to be played and in more or less which order, and make sure you have the necessary facilities for those games. Buy some small prizes for the winners—children love prizes; it almost doesn't matter how small they are, providing everybody ends up winning one by some means or other. And, of course, you have to prepare the food. This should include some of the traditional favourites like cream cakes and chocolate fingers, but children like grown-up sophisticated food and it will give your party an unusual touch if you serve some.

The games suggested in this section are all reasonably easy to organize and should prove successful with children of all ages, both boys and girls. But do remember to ask the child whose party it is what games he or she wants to play, and include them too.

Goose-stepping ■

You will need: a box of chocolates or candy, three lengths of string and a blindfold.

This is a trick game that everyone will enjoy because by the time each player realizes that he or she has been tricked it will be time to enjoy the next player's performance.

Send all the children out of the room, then put a box of chocolates or candy on a high stool as far away from the door as possible. Stretch three pieces of string at increasing heights across the path from the door to the 'treasure'—either tie the ends to chairs or jam them in piles of books.

Bring in the first player and close the door again. Explain that he can help himself to the treasure on the other side of the room if, blindfolded, he can get there without touching the pieces of string. Blindfold him, quietly remove the pieces of string and tell him to start. Egg him on with loud instructions, 'Higher, higher!' 'Nearly there.' 'Go under the next string, down on your tummy now.' Only when he reaches the treasure and removes his blindfold does he discover he has been tricked. In on the joke, he must then join in encouraging the next player.

Games of this kind are just as exciting for the children on the other side of the door, because they are not exactly sure what is going on inside the room and that alone generates excitement.

Other halves ▲■

You will need: safety-pins and a prepared label for each child, each one being half of a well-known name or couple. (e.g. Julius/Caesar, Wyatt/Earp, Dick/Whittington, Romeo/Juliet, etc.) This is a good game for early in the party as it ensures that all the children meet and talk to each other.

Each child has a label pinned to his back and then has to discover both who or what he is and what his other half is. He does this by showing people his label and asking questions—'Am I dead?' 'Am I a person or an animal?' 'Am I real or imaginary?' The only answers can be yes or no. When he thinks he knows what his label says he goes around the room and tries to find the child who is his other half. The first successfully joined halves win. Adults can, of course, amend the names and the rules on what questions can be asked to suit the age-group of the children. Younger children could be told who they are. Then, knowing they are, for example, 'Winnie the' or 'Jack and' they just rush around until they find 'Pooh' or 'the Beanstalk'. And for children who haven't yet learned to read the halves could be drawings—half of a cat, half of a tomato, etc.

Straw racing ■

You will need: a number of straws (the plastic ones are best) cut in half and some short Italian macaroni or any other small objects with holes in them large enough for a straw to go through.

Older children will be best at this game, but even if the littler ones can't do it very well it won't matter much because they will have a lot of fun.

Divide the guests into two teams. Everyone is given a straw to hold in his or her mouth. A piece of macaroni is hooked over the straw of the first child in each team. On the signal to start they have to transfer it—without touching it with their hands—to the straw held by the child next to them. The first team to get the piece of macaroni to the end of the line wins.

Straw racing (left) is a challenging party game as you are not allowed to use your hands.

Artists

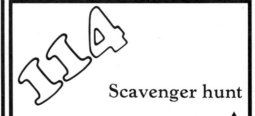

You will need: piles of paper and pencil, and a prepared list of things to draw.

Divide the guests up into two or three teams and give them separate bases as far from each other as possible—in separate rooms perhaps.

Each base should have a chair with a pile of paper and some pencils. The list of objects to be drawn very much depends on the ages of the children, but it is better for them to be too easy than too difficult. The person with the list, preferably an adult, goes to a room as far away from the players as possible. Each team chooses one player to start. They go to see the

adult and are given the first object on the list to draw—things like a table, ladybird, car, tiger, school, spoon, etc., are fine. They run back to their bases and start drawing their object.

The purpose of the game is for each team member to draw objects well enough to be guessed by the other members of his or her team. The artist is not allowed to write any words or to speak—he can only draw and shake or nod his head. When a member of the team thinks he knows what the object is, he runs to the person with the list. If he is wrong he is sent back, if he is right he is given the next object on the list. The team to complete all the drawings first is the winner.

Scavenger hunt

You will need: a list of available objects, one copy for each child.

Each player is given a copy of the list of objects to be collected and a time limit. Obviously the list must be geared to what is available indoors or out.

Rescue

This is not a game to be played if the neighbours are likely to complain about the noise: it starts in complete silence and ends in bedlam.

One child is 'He' and the rest can go anywhere in the house where the doors are open. As soon as 'He' touches another player, that player has to stand still and shout for 'Rescue!' He can't move until another player comes along and touches him, so the smart 'He' hangs around and grabs the others as they attempt a rescue. The game ends when everyone except 'He' is standing stock-still shouting for rescue!

What's the time Mr. Wolf?

You will need: a brown paper bag, scissors and crayons.

This game is guaranteed to be noisy fun, but it does require space. In advance, make a mask from a big brown paper bag, cut two substantial eye holes and draw a wolf's face on it. The player chosen as Mr. Wolf wears the mask. All the other children group in one corner of the room, which is 'home'. Mr. Wolf slowly walks away from them and they follow, asking 'What's the time Mr. Wolf?' Mr. Wolf replies with any time he likes—four o'clock, seven o'clock, three o'clock—but when he says 'Twelve o'clock, dinner time' he turns around to chase his followers. The first one he catches, or the last one home, is the next Mr. Wolf.

No prizes for this game.

I sent a letter to my love

You will need: a letter, and a large enough floor space to seat all the children.

This traditionally popular children's party game is similar to Hunt the Slipper. All the guests except one sit cross-legged in a circle on the floor. The one left is given a 'letter' which she carries as she runs round the outside of the circle reciting: 'I sent a letter to my love, and on the way I dropped it, one of you has picked it up, and put it in his pocket.' Then she taps each child on the head saying 'It isn't you, it isn't you, it isn't you . . .' until finally she drops the letter into someone's lap, saying 'It's YOU.' The child of her choice has to jump up and then both of them run in opposite directions around the outside of the circle to try and get back to the empty place. The one who fails is next to take the letter round.

Find the leader ▲

All the guests but one sit in a circle, cross-legged on the floor. A leader is nominated while the odd man out is outside. When he returns and stands in the middle of the circle, everyone in the circle follows the actions of the leader—clapping hands, banging the floor, standing up, nodding heads, etc. 'He' has to guess who is the leader. When he does so, the leader becomes 'He' and someone else is chosen as leader. (The trick of the game is for the leader to change whatever he is doing only when the the child in the middle's back is turned.)

Treasure hunt ●

You will need: a quantity of small objects to use as 'treasure'.
This game requires preparation before the party starts, but is always exciting and a very good way of starting the party off and breaking the ice. You need to hide the 'treasure' all around the house (or the garden if it is an outdoor party). Shut the doors of the rooms you don't want invaded, and then declare everywhere else fair game. Popular 'treasure' is almost anything small and edible—sweets or candy. Leave the 'treasure' where it is visible, but not obvious. No prizes are required for this type of treasure hunt—the winner eats the most.
Searches for other kinds of treasure— buttons, counters, marbles—deserve a prize for the child who can find most.

Blow feather ●

You will need: a feather or balloon and an empty table top.
Put a light feather or balloon in the middle of a table. Divide the guests

Bang race ■

You will need: five paper bags (or balloons) and one named bag for each guest.
This game needs some advance preparation—collecting all the bags, etc. And don't use balloons unless you are reasonably sure the children are old and strong enough to blow them up.
Each child is given his or her five paper bags. On the other side of the room, or, better still, in another room, there is a line of bags, each marked with the name of a guest. On the word go, the children have to blow up the first of their five bags, burst it, then run and put it in the bag with their name on. They then run back and blow up their second bag and so on. The winner is the first player to have five burst paper bags in the bag with his name on.

Shadows ▲

You will need: a sheet and a very strong light.
Hang the sheet across a room in front of the light. Divide the guests into two teams. The players in one team walk behind the sheet, one at a time, disguising their appearance as much as they can by wriggling, lurching, hunching their shoulders or sagging at the knees. Members of the opposing team have to guess who it is behind the sheet. The team which gets most right is the winner.

into two teams, one on one side of the table and the other opposite. On the word 'Go' each team has to try and blow the feather off the opposite side of the table. One point is scored each time a team succeeds.

Musical dressing ●

You will need: music, a large cardboard box, an old hat, and as many old clothes and trinkets as you can find—hats, socks, scarves, bracelets, cardigans, etc—the more the merrier. Fill the box with the dressing-up material and seat all the guests in a circle around it, one of them wearing the old hat. When the music starts, the hat must be passed round from head to head. When it stops, the player wearing the hat must jump up and put on as many clothes from the box as he can before the music starts again. When the music starts, he must sit down and pass on the hat. The game ends when the box is empty and the winner is the player with the most clothes on. Careful adult handling of the source of music can usually ensure that all the guests get something out of the box.

Silly tea ▲

You will need: about three times as many slips of paper as there are guests, each one with a silly instruction written on it—e.g.: 'Eat this without using your hands.' 'Eat this under the table.' 'Run around the table before eating this.' The more variations you can think of, the more fun for the guests. This is not a wonderful game for the digestion, but then that's not normally a major concern at children's parties. Before the children start eating explain the rules of the 'Silly Tea' to them. That is, each guest has to take one of the slips of paper from a bowl in the centre of the table when he or she wants something to eat and obey the instructions on the slip. The result is a mild pandemonium.
The game can be prolonged by putting the slips back in the bowl or finished by insisting they are not put back.

things to make and

play with outdoors

If you make a sundial (far left) on a sunny day you can keep it and use it to tell the time by throughout the summer—see No. 126

A tin telephone (left) is easy to make and can be used indoors or out —see No. 129

Putting up a simple home-made tent (right) takes very little time and immediately gives you lots of new play ideas—see No. 136.

A good idea for windy weather (above) is to make and fly your own kite— see No. 124

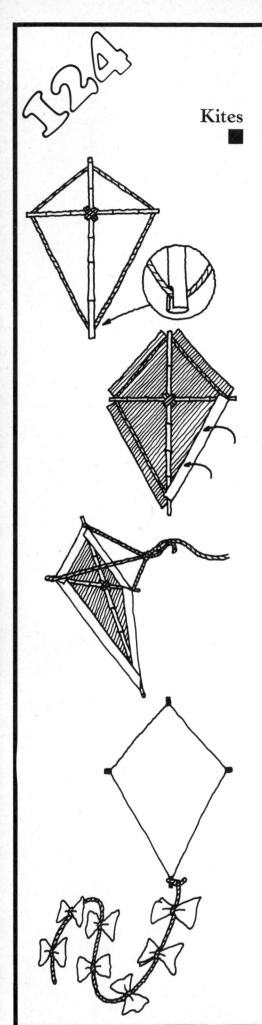

Kites

You will need: a ball of thin, strong string, some lengths of thin bamboo cane, a knife, a sheet of paper or, better still, a piece of fabric—part of an old cotton sheet or an unwanted 'silk' scarf, glue or needle and thread, and pieces of rag or tissue paper.

A kite is one of the oldest toys known to man, and it is still one of the best. And, although they are cheap to buy, there is nothing so satisfactory as making your own kite and getting it to fly. Theoretically, the shape of a kite is unimportant providing that it is balanced and held at a constant angle to the wind. And normally the simpler the shape of the kite the simpler it is to fly.

The size of your kite is dictated only by the size of the paper or fabric and the length of the bamboo—but if you are too ambitious and make a monster you will need a very strong wind to fly it and it will be difficult to handle.

First lay out your paper or fabric and decide what shape you are going to make. The two simplest are the traditional diamond design and the hexagon. If you have a square piece of paper the hexagon will fit on to it better; if you have a rectangular piece, the diamond will fit better.

To make a diamond kite you need just two bamboo canes. Cut one so that it is two thirds longer than the other and bind them tightly together in the position shown in the drawing. Make a cut in all four ends of the bamboo and tie a piece of string all round so that it slots into the ends of the canes.

Lay these bamboo struts on your paper or fabric, and cut around the outer edge, leaving an extra inch all round. Cut a square notch in the corners so that the covering does not overlap the ends of the sticks. Fold over the edge and stick it down securely, or sew it down if the covering is fabric. To make the 'bridle' tie equal lengths of string to the top three corners and knot the ends together so that when they are pulled out the knot is about 12 inches from the covering side of the kite. Make a loop at the knot to attach the kite string.

Finally, tie another piece of string—at least twice as long as the kite—to the bottom of the kite for the tail. Then tie small pieces of rag or bunched-up tissue paper at six-inch intervals along the tail string.

To make a hexagon kite you need three pieces of bamboo cane all the same length. Bind them together in the middle, as shown in the drawing, then make a cut in the ends of the canes and tie a piece of string around the outside, slotting it into the cuts. Lay the framework on to the covering and cut around the edge leaving a one-inch overlap. Cut a notch in all six corners, then stick or sew the overlap down over the string.

The 'bridle' should be fixed from the centre of the kite—make a small hole in the covering and thread the string through—and two adjacent corners. Knot the three strings together about 12 inches from the covering and make a loop for the kite string.

Make the tail in the same way as for the Diamond Kite and tie it at the bottom of a loop of string attached to the two bottom corners.

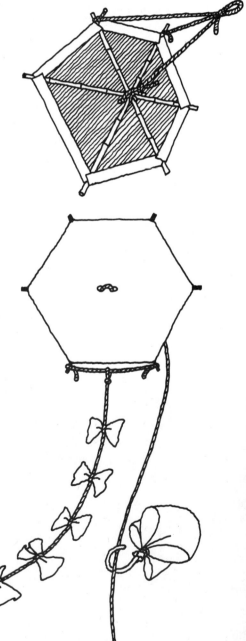

To fly your kite you need a good breezy day. Be sure to choose a place free from trees, electricity pylons or other obstructions. And always wear gloves when flying a kite—if the string slips through your unprotected fingers on a windy day it could cause a nasty burn.

First let out about 30 yards of string and get someone to launch the kite down-wind of you. If there is not much wind about, you will have to run, letting out more string as you go, to get the kite to lift. Once it is up, let the line out slowly as you feel the wind pull.

If the kite sways uncontrollably or if it simply nose-dives towards the ground, it probably means that the towing point on the bridle needs adjusting. Check that the two side lines of the bridle are even; the face of the kite must be at right angles to the string when the string is pulled. If the bridle is properly fixed but the kite still wobbles add more length to increase the stability.

Parachutes or balloons can be sent up the line once you have got your kite flying well. Make a wide hook from a piece of wire and tie it to a balloon or a simple parachute made from a handkerchief. Hook it on the line, jiggle it a little and the wind will take the hook up. When it is near the kite, jerk the line hard to detach the hook and send the parachute or balloon floating to the ground.

126

Sundial

■

You will need: a flat piece of wood 12 inches square, a straight stick 12 inches long, a watch, some glue or nails and some paint.

If you have patience and a clear sunny day you can make your own sundial. Glue or nail the thin, straight stick upright in the centre of the flat piece of wood. Adults must supervise this. If you are going to keep the sundial it needs to be installed in the sunniest position in the garden and nailed to the top of a post sunk in the ground so that it can't move. If you can fix it to the top of a low fence, that is fine.

To make the clock face all you have to do is to wait for a sunny day, then mark the exact position of the shadow cast by the stick on the flat piece of wood every hour. It is best if you can start when the sun comes up and finish when it goes down. Design and paint a nice clock face on the sundial and from then on you will always be able to tell the time from it on a sunny day.

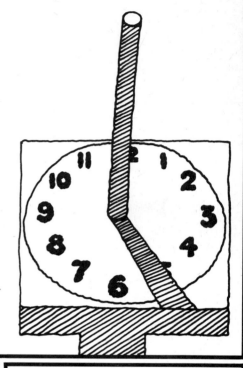

125

Daisy chains

●

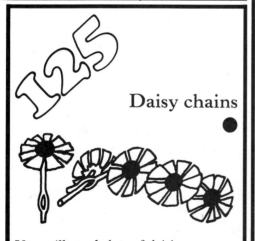

You will need: lots of daisies.

Daisies can be used for the prettiest of all garden 'jewellery'. Pick as many daisies as you can find, making sure they have long stalks. Make a little slit near the bottom of one stalk with your fingernail, then slot another daisy into it. The more daisies you put in, the longer the chain will grow. Make them into loops for necklaces, bracelets or headbands. (You can make chains with buttercups, too, if you can find them.)

127

Scent

●

You will need: the petals of highly scented flowers and a small bottle of water with a screw top.

Collect together the petals of any variety of heavily-perfumed flowers—roses are best. (But don't strip all the flowers in the garden without first asking which ones you must not pick!) Clean the small empty bottle thoroughly, then put in the petals, pressing them in one after the other. When no more petals will go in, fill the bottle with water and screw on the cap. After a few days top up the bottle with more water if necessary. Leave it for about a month with the top screwed down tightly. When you finally open it up, the water should have taken on the same perfume as the petals.

128

Bark rubbing

▲

You will need: a thick, soft pencil, a sheet of paper and four drawing pins [thumb tacks].

Pin the paper on to the trunk of a tree and rub the pencil softly over it so that the pattern of the bark comes through. Stick your rubbings into a nature diary or into a special scrap book and label each one with the name of the tree.

Tin telephones
●▲■

You will need: two empty tin cans without lids and some string.

Make a hole in the bottom of each can, thread the string through and knot it on the inside. When it is stretched tight, messages can be whispered into one tin and heard in the other.

Start with a long piece of string—about 18 ft.—and shorten it little by little until you can hear messages clearly.

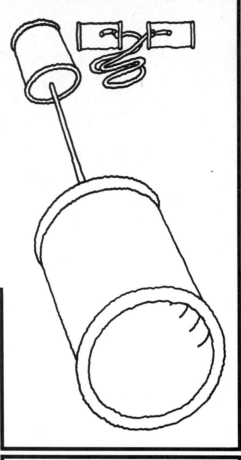

130

Tin can stepping stones
▲

You will need: two tin cans of the same size, string and something to punch holes with.

To start with, punch two holes in the sides of each can near the top. (Parents should do this.) Then thread a long piece of string in a loop through the holes. It should be long enough to stretch from your foot to one hand. Then step on to each of the cans, pull the strings tight and walk away! If there are several of you, you can have tin can stepping stone battles—trying to topple each other off your perches.

131

Bow and arrows
■

You will need: one long, straight branch that will bend without cracking for the bow, a number of thinner straight branches for the arrows (new, green wood is usually better than older branches), a knife and some string.

When you have selected the long branch that will be your bow, cut a groove about one inch from each end. Knot a strong piece of string into one groove, then bend the bow into shape and knot the other end so that the string maintains the shape of the bow. The arrows need to be light and straight, stripped of bark if possible. Make a blunt point at one end and cut a notch at the other so that the arrow will fit snugly into the bowstring. The arrows don't really need feathers or cardboard flights, but if you want to you can make them from stiff cardboard cut to shape and slotted into a cut in the end of the arrow.

Whatever you use as a target (a big cardboard box with target circles painted on it is best) make sure before you fire that there is nothing and no one behind liable to get hurt.

132

Bubbles
●

You will need: a plastic cup, liquid detergent (or soap flakes) and some cooking oil, water, and a bent hairpin or paper clip.

Mix up the bubble solution in a plastic cup—the oil makes your bubbles stronger—then just dip a bent hairpin or paper clip into it. When you take it out some of the solution will stick to it. Blow hard and bubbles will float away in the air.

If you blow the bubbles outdoors on a sunny day, the light shining on them turns them rainbow colours.

133

Twig broom
▲

You will need: a ball of string, a straight branch about $1\frac{1}{2}$ inches thick and $2\frac{1}{2}$ feet long, and as many straight, thin, swishy twigs as you can find.

First tie the string firmly to the thick branch about 8 inches from one end, then arrange some of the twigs round the branch and bind them tightly to it. Add more layers, tying each one into place with string until you finally run out of twigs. Bind the top layer very, very firmly.

This broom is very useful in the garden to sweep up fallen leaves.

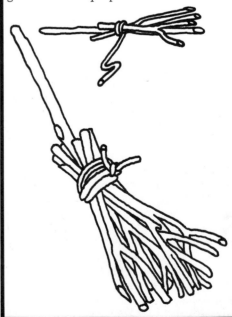

134

Windmills ▲

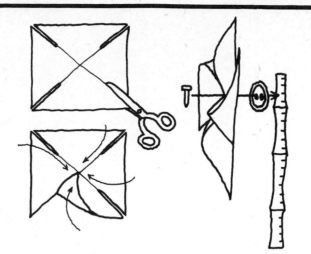

You will need: a square of stiff paper or thin cardboard, a nail or pin, hammer, button, bamboo cane, pencil, ruler, scissors.

Draw two diagonal lines from corner to corner across the square paper or cardboard, then make cuts from each corner towards the centre—the cuts should be half the length of one side of the square. Fold each corner into the centre then press a nail or pin through the centre of the paper, catching in all the corners. Thread the button on at the back and bang the nail into the bamboo cane, taking care to leave plenty of room for the windmill to turn.

135

Twig panels ■

You will need: twigs, a flat piece of wood, sandpaper and glue.

Collect together as many funny-shaped twigs as you can find, particularly old and gnarled ones. Using the natural bends and twists of these twigs to form the letters, see what words you can make.

To make a permanent panel, clean down an old, flat piece of wood with sandpaper, then stick your word down piece by piece with strong glue.

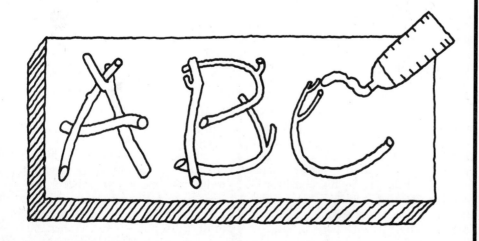

136

Tent ▲

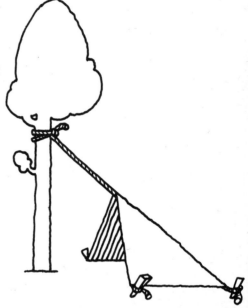

You will need: a length of rope, small branches or tent pegs and canvas or any other available material.

The quickest and simplest way to make a tent is to tie a length of rope (the clothes line is fine, if you can borrow it) to a tree. Throw it over a low branch then peg the other end in the ground about six paces away from the trunk of the tree.

A tent peg is the easiest way to fix the rope to the ground, but you can make a workable peg out of a branch by sharpening one end and cutting a notch in the top to hold the rope.

For the tent itself canvas is best because it won't let in the rain, but failing that most other kinds of material will do. Fold the material into a triangle and place it over the rope, pegging down the corners and the sides if necessary.

137

Twig and branch wigwam ■

You will need: four or five strong, straight branches all about 5 feet long, small branches or twigs, a pair of steps and a length of rope.

Stand the branches in a wigwam shape, borrow a stepladder so that you can reach, and bind them tightly together at the top. (Parents could supervise this stage.) Leave one segment open as the door, and cover the others with small branches and twigs. Start at the bottom and jam them in as tightly as possible, pressing down all the time. Make the walls as thick as possible and the wigwam will be reasonably waterproof.

If you can't find enough twigs, use material and paint it in bold designs.

games to play out-doors

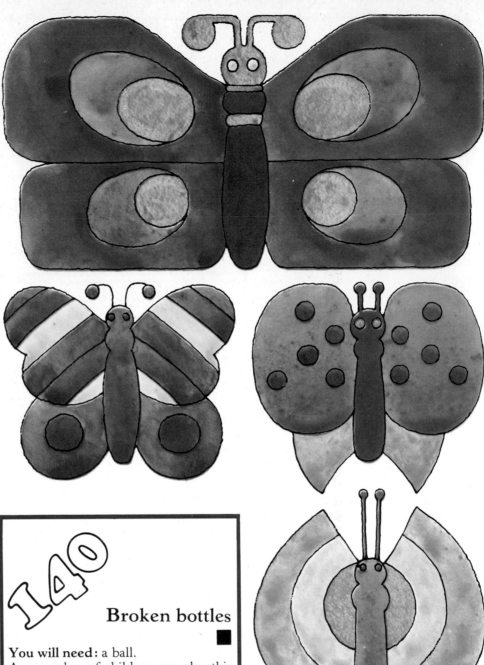

Skittles ●▲

You will need: three small balls and some tin or plastic bottles.
Practically anything that stands on end will serve for makeshift skittles in the garden. Set them up as you would proper skittles. Each player has three balls which can be rolled or thrown at the skittles, depending on how smooth the ground is. The player who knocks over most skittles wins.

Water battle ●

You will need: old plastic detergent bottles and buckets of water.
Save old plastic detergent bottles—they make devastating water pistols for use outside on a warm day.
For a water battle, everyone is given a 'pistol', ammunition is supplied in the form of a couple of buckets full of water and from that moment on it's a free-for-all. (Anyone not wishing to be involved should stand well clear.)

Broken bottles ■

You will need: a ball.
Any number of children can play this popular ball game, providing they are old enough to catch reasonably well. The players stand in a circle and throw a ball backwards and forwards, catching it with both hands. When a player drops the ball he must pay the following penalties: the first time he drops it—he can use only his right hand from then on; the second time—left hand only; third time—he kneels on one knee but uses both hands; the fourth time—he kneels on both knees but uses both hands; the fifth time—still kneeling, but using right hand only; the sixth time—kneeling, using left hand only; the seventh successive time he drops it he is out.
However, every time a player catches the ball while paying his penalties he regains one place until, if he is lucky, he wins back to standing up and catching the ball with both hands.

Butterfly chase ■

You will need: coloured paper, scissors and paper bags.
This needs a little preparation but it is worth it. Lots of butterfly shapes are cut out from coloured paper and hidden round the garden in flowers and on trees etc. All the players are given a paper bag 'net' and the one who catches most 'butterflies' is the winner.

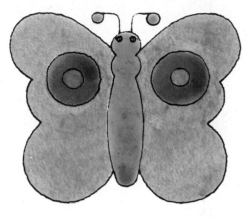

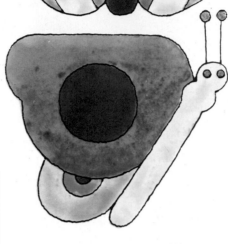

146
Grandmother's footsteps
●▲■

This is an exciting game for children of all ages. One player stands facing a tree or wall with his or her back to all the other children—this is 'Grandmother'. The other players have to stand behind a line some distance away and creep up on the child by the tree without being seen. Every time 'Grandmother' turns her head everyone has to stand absolutely still—anyone 'Grandmother' sees moving is sent back to the starting line. The child to reach 'Grandmother' first becomes the next 'Grandmother'.

142
Fox and geese
●

For this game one child is chosen as 'Mother Goose' and collects all the other children behind her, except one. The odd one out is the 'Fox'. All the rest hanging on to each other's waists behind 'Mother Goose' are the 'geese'. The 'Fox' has to pounce on the last child in the line, and when he does so that child goes behind the 'Fox'. The game continues until all the 'geese' have been turned into 'foxes'.

144
Chain 'He'
▲

This is a good running game for wide open spaces. One child is nominated 'He'. The first player he catches holds hand and they then run as a pair. The next person caught joins on until there is a great sweep of children all trying to catch one last runner.

147
One against the circle
●

This game is ideally played with sets of just four or five children.
One child is 'It' and the other three or four link hands in a circle. The odd child stands outside the circle and points to the player he is going to tag, he then runs round to try and touch that player while the circle spins round in either direction to stop the 'tag' being made. When it is made, the child who was tagged becomes 'It'.

143
Long jump relay
▲

The players divide into two or three teams of the same number of children. The teams then line up behind each other on the 'starting line'. The first member of each team does a standing jump as far as he can. The next player then goes to the exact point on which the leader landed and does a standing jump on from there. The team to reach the furthest point when everyone has jumped is the winner.

145
River of Jordan
▲

You will need: two long pieces of rope. Mark the banks of the river on the grass with the piece of rope. It should be narrow at one end and wide at the other. All the children take it in turns to jump backwards and forwards across the 'River of Jordan', starting at the narrow end. Anyone who fails to make the opposite 'bank' falls out until only one—the winner—is left.

148
Nature treasure hunt
■

If you are out in the countryside, an instructive and amusing game to keep children occupied is a version of the indoor Treasure Hunt.
It is however, a good idea to restrict the area so that no one gets lost, and to impose a time-limit.
Depending upon what time of year it is and what sort of country you are in, everyone goes off—singly or in teams—to collect as many different leaves/flowers/berries/shells as possible.

Gardening is great fun but it does need patience. If you are planning a rock garden (below) remember to leave some gaps to plant things.

With a little encouragement, most children will enjoy gardening, particularly if they can be given their own patch to plant and lay out as they like. Clearly the best plants to choose are the hardy growers—bright, strong flowers like zinnias, marigolds, asters and pansies, and tough vegetables like beans, peas and tomatoes. Older children should be able to grow their entire garden from seed, but for little ones it is probably simpler and more satisfactory to plant seedlings.

Inherent in children's pleasure of being given a patch of garden of their own is the responsibility to look after it. Children over the age of six should be able to care for their gardens by themselves; under that age they will probably need help with the watering and weeding.

149 Seeds

The best way to get seeds for your garden is the way Nature does it—from last year's flowers. If you see any flowers you would particularly like to plant next year in your own garden, wait until they have finished flowering then cut them off at the stalk and hang a bunch up to dry somewhere out of the way indoors. When they are quite dry, take the shrivelled heads to pieces and you will be able to take out the seeds. Put the different seeds into separate envelopes and mark each of them with the name of the flowers. Keep them in a cool, dry place ready for planting in the Spring.

Although some seeds are first planted in a seed box, many of them will grow if they are planted straight into the ground. But, to make quite sure, divide the seeds in each envelope in half and put one half straight in the ground and the rest in a seed box.

Whichever way you do it, you must keep them well-watered. If they sprout up in thick clumps, it is advisable to thin them out gently pulling out the weak seedlings, leaving only the strong, healthy-looking ones.

If you are transplanting seedlings from a seed box to your garden, handle them with great care, press them firmly into the soil and always water them straight away. If you buy packets of seeds, you will find the instructions for planting them on the back.

150 Planning the garden

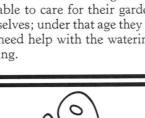

Before you start work on your garden, it is a good idea to decide what you want to do and what you want to grow. Draw a plan on a piece of paper and first draw in any paths, stepping stones or fences that you have decided to have. Draw and colour them so that you can see how it is taking shape. Then draw in position the flowers or vegetables you are going to plant. If this is too complicated, cut out pictures of what you want from seed catalogues and stick them in position like a collage.

151 Initialling a leaf

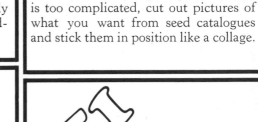

If you do it before the fruit begins to colour you can mark your initials on a flat leaf or your own apple or pear. Cut out your initials from a piece of black paper and stick it to the leaf or fruit. Leave it for about a month, then soak the paper in water and gently lift it off—your initials will show quite clearly in a different colour.

152 Writing with flowers

To make sure everyone knows who owns your garden, you can 'write' your name in flowers. Choose the seeds of very small flowers and divide them up equally for each letter of your name. Rake a small patch of very fine soil, then write your name with a stick in clear letters. Carefully shake the seeds into the grooves, cover them over with soil and keep the patch watered. If you mark out with twigs each area you have planted, you will be sure not to dig up that patch again accidentally.

Long journeys with children need not be an ordeal, but they need some foresight and preparation in order to avoid that risk. Children sitting in the back of a car, or in a boat, train or aeroplane, with nothing to read, nothing to draw with or on, no toys to cuddle, no stimulus of any kind except the outside world flashing by the windows (and not even that when flying) are hardly likely to make ideal travelling companions. An adult might be perfectly happy to sit back and enjoy the scenery; children seldom are.

Most of the games in this section are to be played by two or more children. They can perfectly well be played by only one child but to retain the competitive element in some of them it may be better if an adult joins in.

'Spotting' games can't of course, be played on aeroplanes. And on trains it might not be a good idea to play those games which involve answers being shouted in unison!

The 'Pencil and paper games' (Nos. 162-166) and 'Word games' (Nos. 153-161) can be played anywhere—on trains, boats, aeroplanes or in cars. And some of the car games (Nos. 167-177) can also—with minor alterations—be played in trains.

The best and easiest way to prepare for a long journey with children is to make each of them a 'surprise bag'. The essential contents are lots of drawing paper and colouring materials, preferably crayons. After that, what goes into the bag is largely dependent on the ages and interests of the children. It is not necessary to buy a whole batch of new toys—although a couple of new things will make it that much more exciting. Old toys which have been forgotten or ignored can be saved for a surprise bag and will be welcomed back as old friends. (It is always a good idea to include the favourite toy of the moment, just in case all else fails.) Do not include games or toys made up of little bits and pieces that could get lost en route and, obviously, do not include anything that is so noisy it will distract the driver or other passengers or cannot be easily coped with in restricted space.

Finally, it is well worth keeping the existence of 'surprise bags' as a real surprise—if they know about them in advance they will be bored with them that much faster. Produce them when the initial excitement of a journey begins to pall.

things to do while travelling

A journey seems to pass much faster if you follow your progress on a map.

Initials
▲■

Each child looks out for objects that start with the same letter as his name. The one who can find the most wins.

Who am I?
●▲■

This is a simple guessing game for all the family. While one child covers his ears the rest of the passengers choose an identity for him—someone easy for a little child and more difficult for any older ones. When this has been done, the player with the new identity has to ask questions to try to find out who, or what, he is. The answers can only be 'Yes', 'No' or 'Don't know', so the questions have to be positive—'Am I a real person?', 'Am I an animal?', 'Am I alive?' etc, etc. At the end of a time-limit, imposed by the clock or a certain number of miles travelled, the player has three chances to guess who he is. He scores three points if he is right first time, two if he is right on his second guess, one for the third time and none, of course, if he can't guess.

Mirrors
●

This is a funny game for two children to play. The children face each other. One is a 'mirror' and has to copy everything the other does—funny faces, actions, big smiles, ugly faces, etc. After a while, when one child's imagination gives up or the other becomes tired of being the 'mirror', they change over.

Above or below?
▲

This is a simple quiz for young children of about the same age. The adult calls out the names of a number of vegetables and asks the children to say whether the part which is eaten grows above or below the ground. The first one to answer correctly scores a point. The answers are so often called in unison that it is easy for the adult to arrange for a tie or for a little child who has not been doing too well in previous games to win triumphantly.

Round robin story
■

Someone starts to make up a story and suddenly breaks off in the middle. The next player in the game, without pausing, has to continue the story from there. Then he, too, stops and someone else takes up the tale. The last player has to finish the story off with an exciting finale. This game is funniest if everyone lets his imagination go wild and the story becomes more and more ridiculous.

You don't say
■

Decide on a word that no one must say—the game is most difficult if you choose a very simple word like 'you' or 'I'—and then start an ordinary conversation in which everyone is trying to trick everyone else into saying the forbidden word. Every time it is spoken the culprit loses a point. The winner is the player who has lost least points at the end of a pre-arranged time-limit.

My grandmother went to market
▲■

This memory game can be very amusing, too. One player starts off by saying 'My Grandmother went to market and bought a pound of onions.' The next player says 'My Grandmother went to market and bought a pound of onions and a bag of lollipops.' Each player adds something to the list after repeating what went before. Anyone who can't repeat the complete list in the right order drops out and the winner is the last player left in the game.

I'm thinking of a word
▲■

One player says, 'I'm thinking of a word that rhymes with . . . flea.' The others have to guess what it is within a time-limit and the person who guesses correctly thinks of the next word.

Add an action
▲■

This game will keep children occupied when you are stuck in a traffic jam and the scenery outside hasn't changed for 20 minutes.

Someone starts with an action—something simple, like clapping his hands twice. The next player copies that action and adds one of his own. The next player copies those two actions and adds another. The actions go around and around, the sequence of things to do getting longer and longer. Anyone who misses an action drops out of the game, and the winner is the last player to remember the entire sequence of actions.

Gomuku ■

You will need: pencils and a large sheet of paper divided into squares, a maximum of eighteen down. (If you start off with only a small number of squares, you can add more as you need them.)

This is a Japanese version of noughts and crosses [tic-tac-toe] for two players. One player marks crosses and the other noughts, but instead of drawing them inside the squares, they are drawn on the points where the lines intersect. The object of the game is to get five crosses or five noughts in a straight line in any direction.

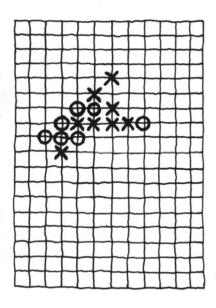

Names ■

You will need: pencils and paper.
This word game is suitable for older children. Each child writes down a christian name, leaving out any duplicate letters. They then have to list as many other names as they can, beginning with each of the letters of the name they first thought of. (The longer the name a child thinks of initially, the more chance he or she has.)

Number maze ■

You will need: pencils and a large piece of paper.
Write 20 pairs of numbers, from 1 to 20, on a large sheet of paper in random positions. Each player takes it in turn to connect a single pair of numbers, but no line may cross any other line. The game gets more and more difficult as it progresses, and the winner is the last person able to draw a line.

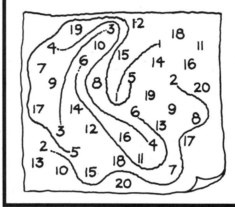

Box nine ■

You will need: pencils and, for each player, sheets of paper with a box divided into nine squares, three across and three down on each one.
The problem is to fill in the boxes with the figures one to nine so that every row, across, down or from corner to corner adds up to fifteen. (See solution page.)

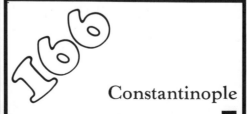

Constantinople ■

You will need: pencils and paper.
Choose a long word and then get each child to write down as many words as possible using letters from the long word. For games of this kind it is best to set a time-limit, say 10 or 15 minutes.

Spotting ▲■

You will need: a list for each child of different things to look out for. (Compile the list to suit the kind of country you are passing through.)
The first child to complete his list—having spotted everything on it—is the winner. To spin the game out, make a rule that everything has to be taken in order, so that each child is only looking out for one thing at a time.

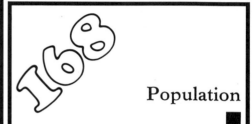

Population ■

This is an amusing game to play if you have got a road guide. You will find population figures listed against most of the entries in the book. So, every time you pass through a town, get everyone to look around and guess how many people live there. The person who makes the closest guess wins. Even little children can play this game once they get some idea of the figures involved—they are just as liable to be right as an adult, and it is a great ego booster for them if they are.

Spell a word ■

You will need: pencils and paper.
Give each child a simple word of the same number of letters to spell and a pencil and paper. Taking it in turns, each child looks for the first letter of his word on the number plate of an oncoming car. As soon as he has got the first letter he moves to the second, and so on. The first child to spell his word is the winner.

Map reading

As soon as they show an interest, children should be encouraged to find out for themselves where they are going, where they are at any given moment and how long the journey will take. Many filling-stations sell cheap maps that are excellent for children, and time invested in explaining what a map is and how it works will be rewarded once a child begins to appreciate its significance.

The first step is to explain the route you are taking. Let the child trace your progress on the map with a pencil and call out the next towns or villages you are due to pass. Then he or she can learn what the various symbols mean and will get great pleasure out of discovering that they really work—that a church, windmill or whatever is where the map says it is.

A budding mathematician can work out average speed by noting the number of miles covered in a quarter of an hour and multiplying by four. If mileages are marked on the map he or she will then be able to work out the approximate time you should arrive at a given point. Learning of this kind is exciting for children and it also makes the journey pass at lightning speed.

171

Blind guessing

Again the driver selects an object a mile or two ahead, a petrol station say or a tall tree, and points it out to the other passengers. Each child then has to close his eyes tightly and shout 'Now' when he thinks they are passing the object.

(To avoid accusations of cheating if there are two players or more it is a good idea if the players all lean forward with their heads on their knees.)

As soon as a child has shouted 'Now' he can sit up and look, but should not make any comment about the accuracy of his guess until everyone has had his or her turn.

Road sign quiz

All the children look out for oncoming road signs and the first to identify a sign correctly scores a point.

Children too young to know most of the road signs are clearly at a disadvantage in this game. Adults can overcome this by asking each child in turn to identify a road sign—scoring a point for a correct answer and nothing for a wrong answer. By careful selection the adult asking the questions can make sure that the younger children are given the easy signs.

173

Guess what I saw?

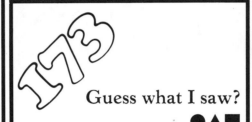

This simple variation of the ever popular 'I Spy', can be played by all the passengers. Someone starts it off by spotting something out of the window and then posing the question 'Guess what I saw?' A few clues, such as size, colour or shape may be given, then everyone has to try and guess what it was within a pre-arranged time limit. If the object isn't guessed, the same player has another turn; if it is, the player who guessed the object then has a turn.

174

Alphabet race

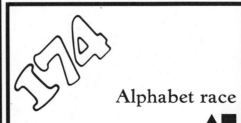

This is a team game or a game for two players.

One team or player looks out of one side of the car and the other team look out of the other side. The object is to spot all the letters of the alphabet in order, starting with A. Letters on road signs, shop signs, advertisement hoardings and car number plates all count. As soon as A is seen the player calls it out and goes on to B. The winning person or team is the one who reaches Z first.

Backseat bingo

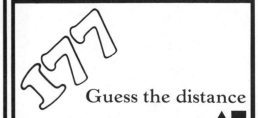

You will need: pencils and a 'bingo-board'—a piece of paper divided into nine squares with a two figure number in each square—for each child.

This game requires at least two children and the participation of an adult.

Give each child a pencil and bingo-board and then call out the last two figures from the number plates of oncoming cars. The first child to cross off all his numbers is the winner. If it is popular the game can be made longer by increasing the number of squares on the 'bingo-board'.

(A good variation to play in trains which does not require adult participation is to substitute the numbers for drawings of animals, trees, bridges, rivers or anything you are likely to pass. Then the children look out for themselves and cross off each picture as they see it.)

176

What's coming next?

This is a good game to play on roads where the traffic is sparse. Each child selects a vehicle and its colour—the winner is the one whose choice comes along first. To string out the game narrow the field by adding the car model (e.g. a black Ford saloon not just a black saloon) or award points for first, second and third and make the first player to get ten points the overall winner.

177

Guess the distance

An object or a place some distance away is selected by the driver and then the child is asked to guess how far away it is. The actual distance is checked on the mileage indicator and the nearest guess wins.

Stable for a Christmas Scene

christmas decorations to make

The Christmas season is one of the most exciting times of the year. It really makes up for the cold weather to know that everyone is planning for a festive time, thinking about presents, and gathering together lovely decorations to make the home bright and welcoming. Since most people now buy their decorations in the shops, some of the more traditional customs are not so familiar. You very rarely see a pretty yule log, with its candle burning brightly, and paper chains that you have made yourself look really charming. Everyone can join in making decorations, and it is a good idea to keep a box full of supplies like sheets of different kinds of paper and card, glitter, ribbon, old Christmas cards, artificial snow, pine cones ect. A final word of advice. When asked to use aerosol sprays, be sure that an adult supervises this stage.

Aerosol sprays should be very easy and convenient to use. However, they have to be handled very carefully. When you are spraying something, you must try to protect the surrounding surface by spreading lots of newspapers, and then placing the object on the paper. Read the instructions on the can of paint before you start, and always spray directly on to the surface you are going to cover; don't wave the can around while you have your finger on the button. Never point the spray in the direction of another person, not only is it hard to remove, but also it could damage their eyes. Never spray near an open flame such as a candle, because the paint is highly inflammable, and when the can is empty, you must throw it away into the bin, never into a fire grate. As long as you keep these safety ideas in mind, you will be quite safe.

Paper chains

●▲

You will need: sheets of different coloured paper, scissors and some glue. The easiest way to make paper chains is to stick loops of paper together, one through the other. You can cut strips to size from coloured paper and glue each one separately, but it will take a long time. It is probably better to buy the strips, ready gummed, in packages. An interesting variation of the traditional paper 'chain' can be made by cutting two long strips of paper, between one and two inches wide. Overlap the ends of each strip so that they form a right angle and glue them together. Then fold the bottom strip over the top strip and repeat the process, glueing more strips on as necessary. Finish by sticking the last fold together. When the chain is opened out it makes an attractive pattern of interlocking paper surfaces.

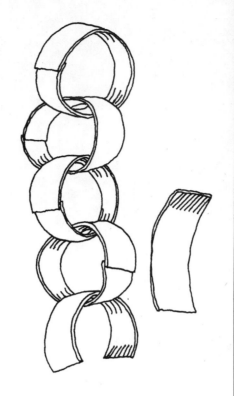

Holly ball

▲■

You will need: papier maché (see game 77), balloon, string, dark green paint, sprigs of holly, sticky tape.

Mix up some papier-maché (see game 77) and cover a large, round balloon with an even layer, leaving a small hole around the knot of the balloon. When it has set hard, burst the balloon with a pin and pull it out. Tie a short piece of string across the hole so that the ball can be hung up. Paint it dark green and when the paint is dry start sticking sprigs of holly all over it. Adhesive tape across the stalks is easiest. Cram as much holly as you can around the ball. If there are not many berries, you can 'fake' them by painting dried peas bright red and sticking them on with glue. When you hang the ball up, make sure it is high enough to stop people knocking into it.

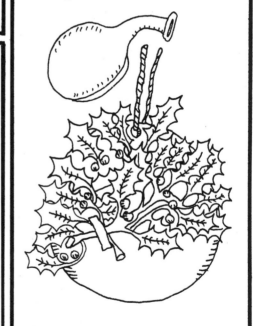

Silver stars and bells

▲■

You will need: stiff silver foil, scissors and thread, pipecleaners, twigs, can of silver aerosol paint.

With a pair of scissors make a number of cuts round the edge of the circle, towards the centre. They could all be about the same distance apart and the same length—no more than half way to the centre. Then, holding the centre of the circle in one hand, give each segment round the edge a twist. Pierce a small hole in the top and pull a piece of thread through to hang the star up.

A simpler way of making conventional star shapes is to draw a pattern on a piece of paper and use it to cut out stars from a sheet of silver foil. The easiest method of drawing a satisfactory star shape is to draw two triangles on top of each other, as shown here.

To make pretty little silver bells, mould a circle of foil over your finger. Put one finger in the centre, then carefully press the edges down. Don't make any sharp points or tears—silver foil can cause a nasty cut if you are not careful. When you are satisfied with the shape, cut the

bottom of the bell straight or give it a scalloped edge. You can make bigger bells by moulding foil over the end of a broom handle.

Use silver stars and bells to help decorate your Christmas tree, or hang them from a circle made from pipe cleaners covered in silver paper. Suspend the whole thing over a table lamp, if possible, and the heat from the bulb will keep it moving and twinkling.

Alternatively, collect a few twigs from the garden and paint them silver—an aerosol can of spray paint is the quickest way of doing it, but be careful to lay out plenty of newspaper because most of the paint will go between the twigs. When they are dry, arrange them in a pot, also covered in silver paper, then hang the stars and bells from the branches.

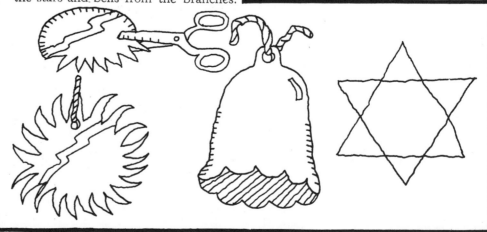

181

Yule log

▲■

You will need: small log split in half or cardboard, brown tissue paper, scraps of bark, cotton wool (absorbent cotton), salt, glue, plasticine, sprigs of holly or mistletoe, acorns, ears of corn, pine cones, evergreen needles, candle.

This has been a traditional Christmas decoration for centuries. Obviously if you can find a real log split in half, it is best to use that. Otherwise make a half log shape from cardboard and cover it with brown tissue paper or, better still scraps of bark. To make the log's 'snow' capping, either use cotton wool (absorbent cotton) or salt. First brush glue along the top of the log, then pour the salt liberally all over it, brushing away afterwards the grains that don't stick. Press a blob of plasticine on the top of the log to hold the decoration, then collect together decorations. Sprinkle them with 'snow' before fixing them into position in the plasticine. Finish off with a candle.

182

Frozen pond

▲■

You will need: small piece of mirror, cotton wool (absorbent cotton), pine sprigs, fir cones, salt, plasticine. To make this centrepiece for the Christmas table you need a small piece of mirror, to represent the frozen surface of a pond. Edge the pond with fluffy cotton wool (absorbent cotton) and make snow-capped trees from tiny sprigs of the Christmas tree. Fir cones, if you can get them, make convincing 'bushes' if sprinkled with salt and stood on end in a blob of plasticine. It is fun to stand toy figures on the ice.

183

Advent calendar

▲■

You will need: two sheets of thin cardboard the same size, old Christmas cards, glue, scissors.

This is fun to make because it shows how close Christmas Day is. The idea of an advent calendar is that every day from the first to the 25th of December you open a little flap in the calendar to expose a different picture.

To make one, first of all draw 25 boxes on one sheet of cardboard, all the same size except one, which should be bigger than the others—this is the one you open on Christmas day. Divide each box in half, vertically, then very carefully cut along the dividing line and the top and bottom edges of the box. This will make two little 'doors' to open. Fold them all back then put this sheet of cardboard over the second sheet and mark the positions of the boxes with a pencil.

Next, cut out pictures from old Christmas cards and stick them onto the second sheet of cardboard in the position of the boxes. If you can, find little pictures, or parts of pictures, that fit the size of the boxes. When that is done, close all the flaps on the other piece of cardboard and carefully paste the back of this sheet, all round the edge and between the flaps. Stick the two sheets together. Number each flap from one to 25, then decorate the front with drawings of Christmas trees or holly or any seasonal pictures you like. Make two holes in the top of the calendar and tie a piece of string or wool through them so that you can hang the calendar up. Open one a day from December 1. And no cheating.

184

Egg-box stars

▲■

You will need: eggbox, scissors, glue, can of aerosol silver paint.

Cut the cone sections from an eggbox. Then, with a pair of sharp scissors, make V-shaped cuts round the sides of each cone so that you are left with pointed 'petals' all round the edge. You will need about ten to make a complete star. Using a strong, quick-setting glue, stick them together back to back so that the spiky points are all sticking out. Spray with silver paint.

185

Fairy castle

▲■

You will need: six empty round containers (detergent bottles will do), thick cardboard, matchsticks, coloured paper, aerosol paint in silver or gold, cotton wool (absorbent cotton), glue, scissors.

Collect together half a dozen empty, round containers—the taller and thinner the better. Stick them in a cluster onto a piece of thick cardboard. These will be the castle. Make nice pointed roofs from circles of cardboard and stick them on the tops of the containers. Flags made from matchsticks and paper stuck into the points of the roofs will make the castles more interesting. When you have finished all the building, spray the whole lot, cardboard base and all, with silver or gold paint. Make sure you protect the background before you start. When the spray paint is dry, paint in the windows and doors with black paint. Make clouds with cotton wool (absorbent cotton).

186

Christmas window

■

You will need: stiff paper, coloured tissue paper, scissors, glue.

In Scandinavia, some families decorate windows with cut-out snowflakes, seasonal motifs and snow scenes, made of coloured papers and foils. The windows look pretty from both inside and outside, particularly when the shapes are cut in transparent materials. Make the Nativity Christmas window in coloured tissue paper which will give a charming stained glass effect. The diagram gives a shape for a tree, a figure which can be adapted to make the Wise men, the Shepherds and the Holy Family, a sheep, a crown, a hat and the Christ Child. Draw the shapes on to stiff paper, cut out, and then cut the tissue paper out round the outline.

Use a clear adhesive for glueing the shapes on the glass and overlap some of them for a striking effect. Don't use this on a damp window.

Here are the seven shapes which make up the Nativity window; a tree which is cut out on the fold; a figure, to adapt for the three Wise Men, the Shepherds, Joseph and Mary; the Christ Child in swaddling clothes and a sheep. Three different kinds of headwear are given. Follow the lines shown in the key below for each shape.

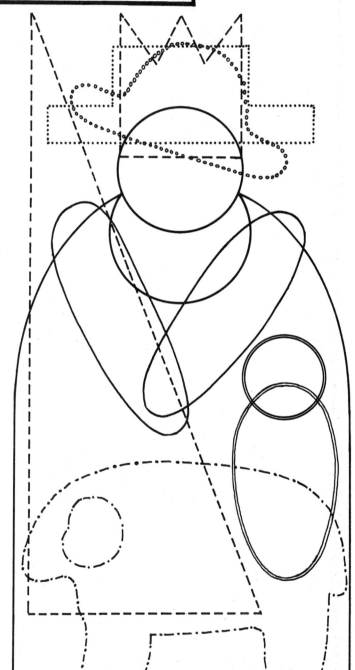

— — — tree, crown   —·—·— sheep

———— person   ═════ child

·········· hat A   ∘∘∘∘∘∘∘ hat B

Tree decorations

▲■

You will need: magazines, pieces of felt, cardboard, beads, buttons, sequins, scraps of lace and braid, fir cones, twigs, nutshells, leaves, glitter dust, glue, gold water paint, thread, scissors. Christmas tree decorations are more fun if they're home-made and everyone can join in the making. Cut shapes out of cardboard—some are illustrated but trace some more from book and magazine illustrations. Cover the shapes with felt, inserting a small loop of thread before glueing.

Decorate the shapes lavishly with beads, buttons, sequins, scraps of lace and braid. Dab adhesive on some areas and sprinkle glitter dust on to them. Another easy-make for you to try. Collect fir cones, twigs, dried leaves, wishbones, nutshells and egg-shells. Paint with gold water paint and sprinkle with glitter dust before the paint dries.

gifts to make for christmas

Everyone will appreciate a gift that you have made yourself. Here are a few ideas you may like to try, none of them are difficult.

188 Trinket box ∎

You will need: a small, strong cardboard box with a separate lid, coloured paper, shells, pebbles, decorations, can of aerosol varnish paint.

To decorate the box, you must use your imagination to make the most of what is available. Tiny shells (if you live near the seaside) look very pretty, but lots of little round pebbles picked up from the garden can be equally attractive. Stick them on the top and sides of the lid, then spray with clear varnish to give them a sheen. Cover the bottom part of the box with coloured paper, or paint it a bright colour. You can try other decorations too.

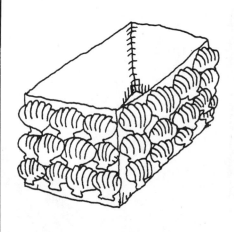

189 Wall tidy ∎

You will need: stiff cardboard, coloured paper, cardboard cartons, string, glue, scissors.

Cover a large square or rectangle of stiff cardboard with coloured paper or a piece of old wallpaper. Punch two holes in the centre on the top edge and thread a piece of string through to hang up the wall tidy when it is finished. Next find some empty cardboard cartons, cut the top flaps off and cover them in matching paper. Stick them on the backing board so that they can be used for holding pencils, paper and odds and ends. Finish off the decoration by sticking on tissue flowers.

190 Snail egg cosy ∎

You will need: two pieces of felt 8 inches square, needle, thread or wool, glue, scissors.

Practise drawing the snail shape on a piece of paper, then cut out a pattern—but make sure first of all that the 'shell' part of the snail will be big enough to cover an egg and keep it warm. Using the pattern as a guide, cut the shape from the two pieces of felt. Draw a spiral on the 'shell' and sew over it in coloured cotton or wool. Then, using a fabric glue like Copydex, stick the two pieces of felt together along the head, round the top edge of the shell and along the tail. Sew on eyes and mouth.

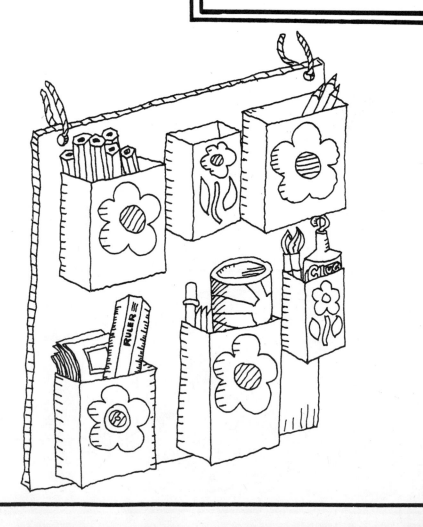

Table mat
●▲

You will need: cardboard, paper doilies, glue, coloured paints, scissors.
An easy way to make pretty table mats is to use paper doilies stuck onto cardboard. Cut out circles of cardboard the same size as the doilies and paint them in bright colours. When the paint is dry, stick the doilies on. The colour underneath will show the pattern.

Calendar collage
▲■

You will need: small calendars, cardboard, plain paper, glue, decorations (fabric, rice etc), ribbon, scissors,
Small calendars to hang underneath a nice picture are very cheap. Buy three or four and then set about making the pictures to go above them. You need a piece of stiff cardboard about 10 inches by 12 inches. Cover it with a piece of plain paper, then draw a simple picture on it. Decide what you have got available to make the collage—scraps of fabric, sand, sequins, pasta, rice (see 85-94 for more collage ideas). If you are using loose material, carefully paste the area of the picture you want to cover, and then pour the material on to it, brushing away the bits that haven't stuck. If you are using fabric or coloured paper, carefully cut it to size then stick it into place. The simpler the picture you draw the easy it will be to make it into a good collage.

Party centre-piece
■

You will need: two cardboard boxes with flaps, chocolate beans, Gesso (plaster of Paris), coloured transparent paper or cellophane, adhesive tape, scissors, glue.
This makes a lovely surprise for a Christmas party centre-piece. To make it, first cut the shapes of the gables from the flaps at each end of the box. Cut the roof from the other box, with a hole for the chimney stack as shown in the illustration (below). Glue the roof in place. Next insert a small box in the hole, securing it with adhesive tape. Make a chimney with a small tube of paper. Cut windows with shutters in the sides; cut the door to stand open at one end, and cut holes for the gable windows. Mix the Gesso to a fairly stiff paste, and spread it over the house. Then, before it dries, press the chocolate beans into the surface to make a a nice pattern. You may like to sprinkle glitter over the house to make it really festive. To finish off, cut squares of transparent paper or cellophane to size, and stick them neatly on the inside of the windows.

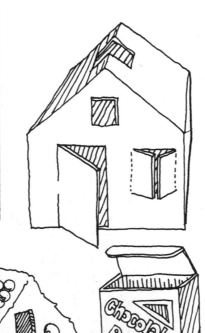

Pomander
■

You will need: an orange, 1½ yards brown cord or velvet ribbon, packets of cloves, allspice and cinnamon.
A traditional present to give at Christmas, pomanders have a beautiful spicy scent, and are hung in the wardrobe. Begin by making channels for the cord using cloves. To form first horizontal groove, press two parallel lines of cloves. right round orange, leaving space for cord between them. Form a second groove in the same way, at right angles to the first. The orange now has four quarters outlined, fill these with cloves, Tie cord round orange.
Hang in a dry place, such as an airing cupboard for a week or two, to allow orange to dry out. Next make a mixture of equal parts of allspice and cinnamon. Sprinkle over pomander, wrap lightly in a cloth and keep in airing cupboard for another week.

Decorated mugs

▲■

You will need: soak-on transfers, mugs or plates, scissors, tissues, clear polyurethane varnish, brush.

These are colourful gifts to make for your friends, and can be used for storing pens, as flower holders, or simply for decoration.

Clean the surface of the plate or mug thoroughly, making sure that it is quite dry and free from grease.

Cut out each transfer separately and soak each one for about a minute in warm water. Place it in position and, while holding the white non-transfer paper between finger and thumb, very gently slide the picture on to the mug. As the transfer is still movable until it dries out, you can adjust the transfer as you wish. Blot off the surplus water

If you wish to make the transfers completely waterproof, wait until they are thoroughly dry and then paint over the picture with a thin coat of clear polyurethane varnish—but remember that utensils treated in this way are for decoration only.

Coloured stones

▲■

You will need: collection of smooth, clean, stones of different sizes, water colour or poster paints, thick and thin brushes, fixative spray or clear nail varnish, felt-tipped pens in different colours.

A collection of stones which you have found and decorated yourself is lovely to give as a gift. They make pretty paper-weights, or just as nice, they can be used as a decoration, arranged in a pile.

First scrub stones clean and dry well. Paint stone with two coats of poster paint, unless you are using the actual colour of your stone as a background, then carefully paint patterns. Leave stone to dry, then spray with fixative (artists use this to prevent drawings from smudging), it does the same for stones but does not make them waterproof. If you like, you can use clear nail varnish.

An alternative is to use felt-tipped pens instead of poster paint. The illustration above will give you lots of ideas.

String box

Felt flowers

Wrapping presents

You will need: a round cardboard drum with a lid, big enough to hold a ball of string, glue, paint, ball of string.

Firstly make a hole in the middle of the lid, then paint both the lid and the top part of the drum in a nice bright colour. Buy a ball of string to go inside, but you can use some of it to decorate the outside of the drum. Smear a strong glue all over the sides of the drum up to about half an inch below the lid. Then, starting at the bottom, wind the string round and round the drum so that it completely covers the glued area. When you have reached the top, cut the string off and press the end firmly into the glue. Wipe away any excess glue. Thread the end of the ball of string through the hole in the lid, put the ball in the drum and replace the lid. The box also looks good if the string is wound round in inch-wide bands instead of all the way up. To do it this way, paint the whole of the drum first and when the paint is dry apply the glue only to the bands where you want to stick the string.

You will need: felt pieces, cotton wool (absorbent cotton) fine wire, green crêpe paper, fabric glue, thread, scissors These pretty felt flowers make a super gift for mother, who may pin them to a hat.

Cut out the felt into small ovals or petal shapes. Take a length of wire, about four inches (or longer, depending on the length of stem you require), and wind a strip of cotton wool around one end. Place a few petals round the wool, and tie firmly with cotton thread.

Cut the crêpe paper into strips and wind round the wire to make the stem. Using the fabric adhesive, add the rest of the petals one by one to the few already in place. Moisten the outer edges of the petals and gently bend them outwards for a realistic effect.

You will need: Christmas wrapping paper, brown or white paper, scissors, can of aerosol silver paint, coloured ribbons.

The more attractive your presents look when they are wrapped the more pleasure they will give. Bright Christmas wrapping paper is very cheap, so it is hardly worth making your own. However, if you are determined, very pretty Christmas wrapping can be made from ordinary sheets of brown or white paper. Lay the paper flat on the floor with plenty of newspaper underneath it. Then cut circles of different sizes from a sheet of thin white paper. Fold each circle in half twice, then make little notch cuts all round the edges with a pair of sharp scissors. When you open the circles out, they will look like snowflakes. Flatten them so the creases disappear and lay them out on the paper on the floor. Using an aerosol can of silver paint, lightly spray the paper all over. Lift the 'snowflakes' when the paper is dry and their outlines will have left an attractive pattern. Look at the diagrams for some ideas for wrapping different shapes. If you have a difficult shaped present to wrap up, you will find it easiest to stand it on a sheet of wrapping paper, then gather the edges all round and tie them with a piece of coloured ribbon.

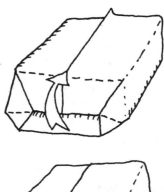

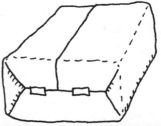

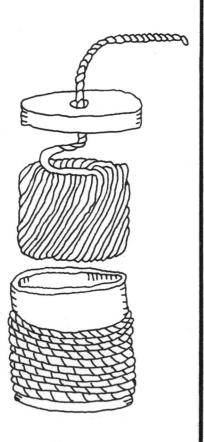

Always finish off the wrapping with a big bow, if you have some ribbon, and try to make the shape of the parcel quite different from the shape of the present so that no one can guess what is inside!

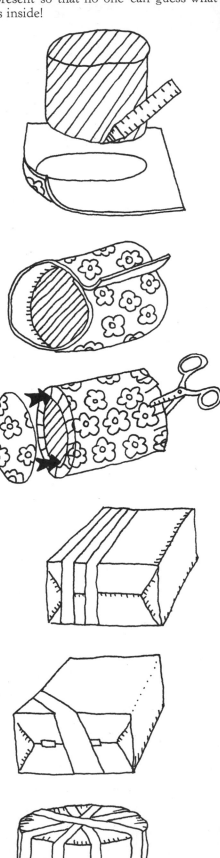

christmas cards to make

If you can mass produce your Christmas cards you will find it much easier to make them for all your friends and family. Making a number of cards in a batch takes more time and trouble in preparation, but it is worth it in the end.

Thin cardboard is obviously best for making Christmas cards, but if you can't find enough an ordinary sheet of paper folded in half twice makes a card that will be stiff enough to stand up.

200

Three kings

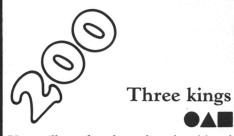

You will need: coloured card, gold and silver paper, scissors.

From the gold paper, cut out the shape of crowns—if you put a number of sheets together you will be able to cut out three or four crowns at a time. Using the same technique, cut out stars from the silver paper. Stick three crowns on each card, to represent the star that guided them to the stable at Bethlehem. Don't add anything else to the card—it is most effective if it is kept simple.

199

Cracker card

You will need: thin card, coloured pencils or crayons, scissors.

On a rectangular piece of card draw a bursting cracker, like the one shown here. You can draw a little Father Christmas tumbling out or pictures of toys or write 'Happy Christmas' in nice lettering. When the drawing is complete, fold the card over so that only a whole cracker shows from the front. It 'bursts' when the card is opened.

These super cracker surprise cards are nice to make with special messages for your friends or members of your family. Everybody will be delighted that they have a personal card.

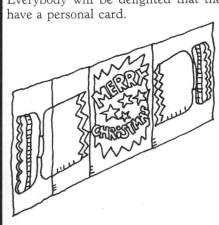

Christmas tree ▲■

You will need: blank cards, some bright green paper, some bright red paper, scissors and a couple of packets of adhesive silver stars (obtainable from any stationers).

Draw a simple outline of a Christmas tree on the green paper and a big tub on the red paper. Cut them out and stick them into position onto the cards. Then cover the tree with little silver stars to represent fairy lights.

To make a three dimensional Christmas tree that will stand up by itself, draw the shape of a tree and tub combined on a piece of thin card—don't make the trunk of the tree too narrow. Put another piece of cardboard underneath it, then cut round the outline, cutting both pieces together. Colour both sides of both pieces of card—green for the tree, red for the tub, and stick on some silver stars if you have got some. Then make a cut down the centre of each tree, half way along its length. Start at the bottom with one tree and the top at the other. Slot these two cuts together and the tree will stand upright.

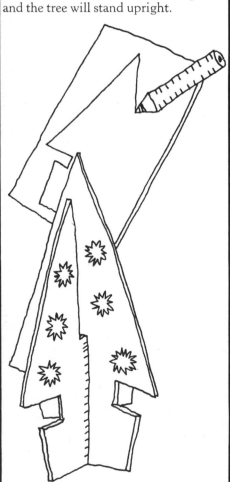

Snowflakes ■

You will need: old newspaper, thin card, can of silver aerosol paint, scissors.

Lay out a number of blank cards on several sheets of old newspaper and give them a coat of silver paint with an aerosol spray. Cut out circles of white paper a little smaller than the cards and fold them in half, twice. Cut notches all round the edges and open them out to make a snowflake pattern. Stick one on each of the silver cards, when dry.

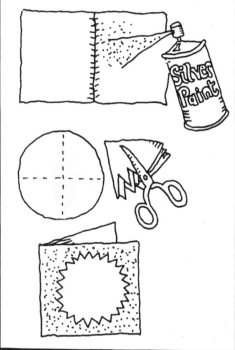

203

Glitter cards ●▲■

You will need: pot of 'glitter', glue, thin card.

A pot of 'glitter' will add sparkle to your Christmas cards. You can buy it at Christmas time for most stationers. An effective way to use it is by writing 'Merry Christmas' on a blank card with a brush soaked in glue. While the glue is still wet, sprinkle the glitter all over the card, leave it for a few minutes then gently shake off the glitter that has not stuck onto a clean sheet of paper so that you don't waste any. It will look best on a card of dark coloured paper.

Stable scene ■

You will need: one shoe box, two empty match boxes, piece of stiff card, piece of corrugated cardboard, piece of chipboard about 12in square, glue, scissors, pencil, straw, modelling clay.

Cut a piece of stiff card 2in wider than one long side of the shoe box. Cut away one long side of the box, and glue the card to one long side, to make a 2in flap. To make the roof, cut the edges off the lid of the box, leaving one long edge as a flap. Glue this flap to the back of the card, so that it slopes forward. To make supporting posts, wrap some card around the pencil, and glue firmly into tubes. Then position them under roof, and cut at an angle to fit. Glue to the roof.

To make the walls, cut two pieces of corrugated cardboard in L shapes, and trim to fit the slope of the roof. Glue to the sides of the box, then curl the front edges around the posts and glue. Cut a piece of corrugated card large enough to overlap the box by $\frac{1}{2}$in in the front, and $\frac{1}{4}$in on the sides. Glue to the roof, and glue on straw to make a thatch. To make the stalls, wrap two strips of corrugated card around the matchboxes so that they overlap the top, and glue. Glue the stalls in the corners of the stable, and glue the stable to the chipboard. Scatter straw around, and arrange little nativity figures and animals, which you can buy or make from modelling clay.

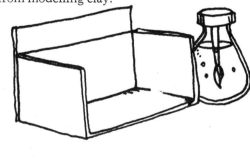

gifts to make for easter

The most traditional gift to give for Easter is a decorated egg, and here are some really super designs for you to try. Also why not make a pretty Easter card, or a special posy of Spring time flowers in a lacy doily.

Decorated eggs
▲■

You will need: eggs, wooden egg cups, fine paint brushes, enamel paint in bright colours, felt-tipped pens in bright colours, clear glue, buckwheat, tiny dried flower heads or small coloured beads, onion skins, polyurethane varnish, latex-based adhesive, thread.

The most traditional gifts to make for Easter are decorated eggs, and here are lots of really super ideas to make them look beautiful. Try a decorated egg in a matching egg cup. Hard-boil your egg, and place it in an egg cup that fits it snugly. You may like to glue it in place.

Pencil your design on to the egg, and continue it on to the cup. Then fill in your pattern with enamel paint or with the felt-tipped pens.

You can make lovely textured eggs by first hard-boiling them. Then give each egg a thick coat of adhesive, and roll in a plate of buckwheat until it is completely covered. When dry, decorate the egg with the dried flower heads or with the beads.

Another pretty way to colour your eggs is to create a marbled effect. To do this, wrap the eggs in onion skins (the brown outer skin of the onion), and then bind them tightly with thread. Wrap each egg in a rag, and boil for half an hour. You'll be amazed at how pretty they are. Finally, give all your decorated eggs a thin coat of polyurethane varnish.

Easter cards
●▲■

You will need: thin card, two coins, one small, one large; scissors, pencil, paint or coloured crayons.

Here are two sorts of Easter cards to make. First, cut a piece of card and fold in half. Then take your two coins, and draw around them to make either a chick or a rabbit as shown in the drawings. Then draw eyes, ears, tails, beaks etc, paint the card or colour with crayons, and write an Easter message inside.

Easter posy
▲■

You will need: a paper doily, a pretty selection of small spring flowers like primroses, daisies, etc; some thin wire, green paper, ribbon.

Make a little hole in the centre of the doily, and thread the stalks of the flowers through the hole. When you are satisfied with the shape and size of the posy, wrap the wire gently around the stalks, and cover them with the green paper. To secure the posy, tie around a big bow of ribbon.

tasty gifts to make

Those of you who are allowed to do some cooking already will know how careful you have to be, especially when using a stove. The best way to be sure is to ask an adult to supervise when you are heating anything. Always make sure that your hands are clean, and try to wash up as you go along. The presentation of gifts is very important, so try and make a collection of pretty jars, bottles and boxes, and label gifts neatly.

208 Bouquets garnis

You will need: eight bayleaves, four teaspoons of dried thyme, four teaspoons of dried marjoram, four teaspoons of dried parsley. A piece of cheesecloth cut into eight circles, each six inches in diameter, thread, scissors. Cut the cheesecloth into circles, place a bayleaf in the centre of each piece and add a half teaspoon each of the other herbs. Gather the cheesecloth round the herbs to form a bag, and secure tightly with the thread, leaving long ends. This makes eight bouquets garnis, but if you want to make more, simply multiply the quantities. Store them in a really pretty container, and make a nice label. Anyone you know who loves cooking will be delighted with this simple gift.

209 Herb butters
▲■

You will need: one pound of butter, at room temperature, juice of half a small lemon, four tablespoons of chopped fresh herbs—you can use mint, sage, parsley, tarragon; a pretty container like a jar with a lid.

Choose which herb you are going to use to flavour your butter. Cream the herbs, butter and lemon together very thoroughly, then press into a cool stone jar. Make a pretty decoration on the surface with a fork or a butter pat. Herb butters will keep in the refrigerator for a week.

210 Herb oils and vinegars
▲■

You will need: four or five sprigs of fresh tarragon, mint or thyme, one pint (two and a half cups) of good olive oil, or if you are making herb flavoured vinegar, the same quantity of wine or cider vinegar; clean glass bottle or tall glass jar, with tightly fitting lids.

Choose which herb you are going to use. Do not remove the leaves, but rub them between your fingers till you can smell the scent of the herb very strongly. Place the herb in your container, then fill it with the oil or vinegar. Finally, seal with a tightly fitting cork or lid. Leave it for at least a month before it is ready to use. The herbs look very pretty floating in the containers.

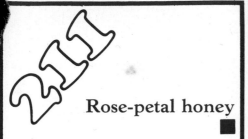

Rose-petal honey ■

You will need: 12 fresh, strongly scented cabbage roses (ask permission before you pick them); four tablespoons water, one pound of clear honey, clean sterilized jar or pot, heavy-bottomed pan.

This is a delicious and easy to make gift for the summer time. To make it, remove the petals from the flower heads, making sure they are all in perfect condition. Place them in a colander, and sprinkle with a little cold water to make sure they are quite clean. Put them in a heavy bottomed pan, and place the pan over very low heat. Stir continuously for five minutes. Next, pour on the honey, bring the mixture to the boil, cover with a lid, turn down the heat and simmer for 30 minutes. Strain off the rose petals, and pour the deliciously scented honey into your jar or pot, and seal it tightly. Make a pretty label, and finish with a nice ribbon.

Butterscotch fudge ■

You will need: eight fluid ounces (one cup) sweetened condensed milk; one pound castor (two cups of fine) sugar; two ounces (four tablespoons) butter; a few drops of butterscotch essence; four tablespoons water; heavy-bottomed pan. Spread the bottom of the pan with butter, and place all the ingredients in it. Warm over low heat, stirring continuously until the sugar has dissolved. Bring the mixture to the boil, and continue boiling for ten minutes. Remove the pan from the heat, and beat the mixture hard until it is thick.

Chocoloate truffles ■

You will need: eight ounces of plain (semi-sweet) chocolate, three tablespoons unsweetened evaporated milk, one teaspoon of vanilla essence, four ounces icing (one cup confectioners') sugar, a little chocolate vermicelli (sprinkles) and a little dessicated (shredded) coconut, mixing bowl, saucepan. Chop the chocolate into small pieces, and melt it slowly in a bowl over a saucepan of hot water. Don't heat it too much, just to melting point. Stir in the evaporated milk, the vanilla, and the sugar, remove from the heat, and let it cool slowly. Shape the mixture into small balls, and coat half with the vermicelli (sprinkles) and the rest with coconut. Leave the sweets (candies) to harden, then gift-wrap prettily.

This will take several minutes, and is very important or the fudge will not set. Turn the mixture into a buttered tray, and leave it in the refrigerator or a cool place to set. When it is ready, cut it into evenly sized squares, and pack it into a pretty presentation box, which you can decorate.

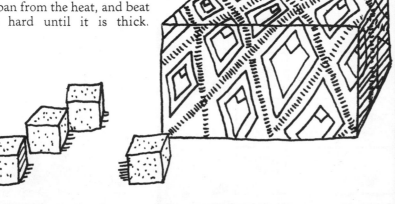

Coconut ice ▲■

You will need: one large can of condensed milk, 12 ounces icing (three cups confectioners') sugar, six ounces dessicated (one and a half cups shredded) coconut, a drop of cochineal, mixing bowl.

Mix together the condensed milk and the sugar. Stir in the coconut, (the mixture should be very stiff) and divide into two portions. Tint one half of the mixture pale pink with the cochineal. Shape the mixture into two bars and press firmly together. Dust a baking sheet with icing sugar and leave the ice until firm. Cut into squares, and then gift wrap it in the nicest box you have.

Fondant peppermint creams ▲■

You will need: one pound icing (four cups confectioners') sugar; one egg white; one teaspoon of lemon juice; a few drops of peppermint essence; rolling pin, mixing bowl. Shake the sugar through a sieve into the mixing bowl. Add the egg white, lemon juice and peppermint essence, and stir with a wooden spoon until all the ingredients are thoroughly mixed together. Then turn the mixture onto a board dusted with a little more of the sugar, and carefully roll out to ¼in thickness, using a sugar-coated rolling pin. Cut the mixture into small circles, and leave to dry out overnight on a wire rack. If you like you can make different coloured creams by adding a few drops of food colouring to the mixture. Pack them neatly into a pretty box, decorated with ribbons etc.

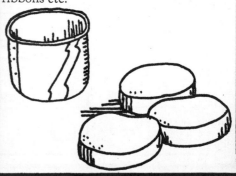

solutions

44

Swapping

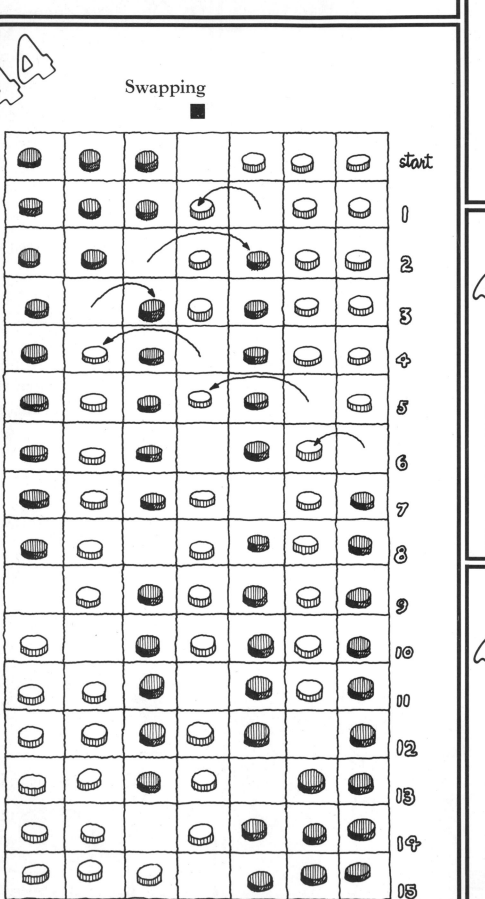

start
1
2
3
4
5
6
7
8
9
10
11
12
13
14
15

45

Separate circles

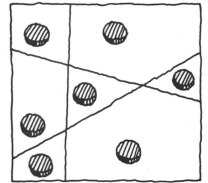

103

Draught-board puzzle

165

Box nine

2	9	4
7	5	3
6	1	8

more printing ideas

More printing ideas

Delightful pictures like the one opposite can be created by using all sorts of materials as well as leaves to print from. For example you can use bits of bracken to make trees, pieces of sponge to make clouds, pieces of fabric for different textures, thread and pieces of cardboard to make fences—in fact anything which has an interesting texture. You should experiment as much as possible, and build up pictures as they occur to you. The printing method is basically a matter of covering your material with thick poster paint, and then pressing it firmly on to the surface of your picture.

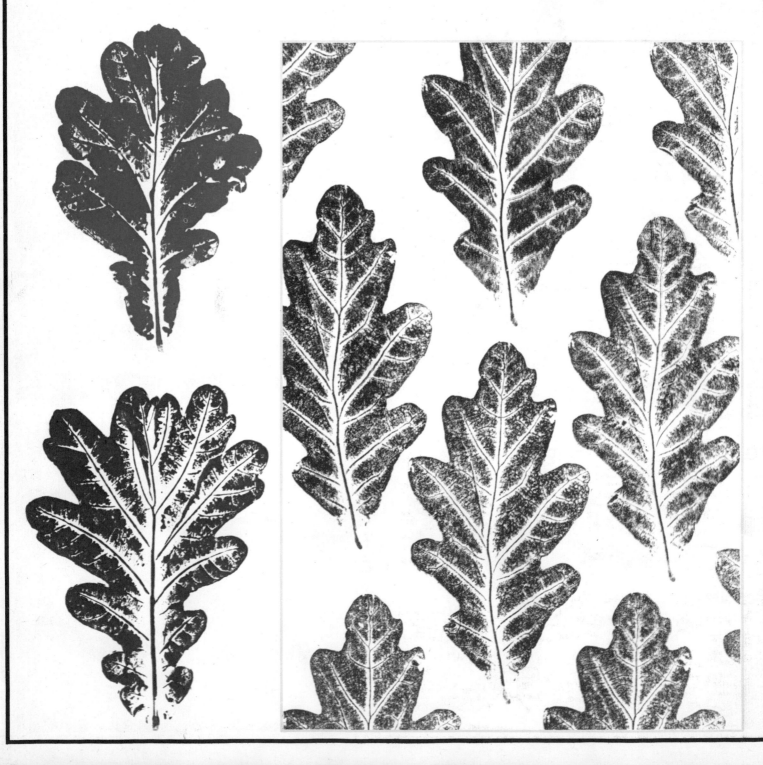